TEXAS DISASTERS

Praise for the Books of Mona D. Sizer

Texas Bandits: Real to Reel

"Her best book yet as she combines a delightful sense of humor and a passion for her subject. . . ."
—Eileen Mattei, *Valley Morning Star*

Texas Money: All the Law Allows

"Get a copy of *Texas Money*. You will enjoy the stories of the rich."
—Jerry Turner, *Mexia Daily News*

"Sizer offers a glimpse into extraordinary lives of those who have acquired legendary wealth."
—Barnes and Noble *Events*

Texas Politicians: Good 'n' Bad

"An anecdotal lark through state shenanigans."
—Jan Upton Seale, *Texas Books in Review*

Texas Justice: Bought and Paid For

"For those who love true crime, here it is with a Texas twist. An engrossing read."
—Doris Meredith, *The Round-up*

Texas Heroes: A Dynasty of Courage

"Sizer has chosen men from Texas history to identify as heroic and courageous. Very readable."
—Chuck Parsons, *True West*

The King Ranch Story: Truth and Myth

"Sizer brings the first meeting of King with his future wife to life like a screenplay, or a James Michener novel."
—Jim McKone, *The Monitor*

"The Queen of Texas Pop History"
—Eileen Mattei, *Valley Morning Star*

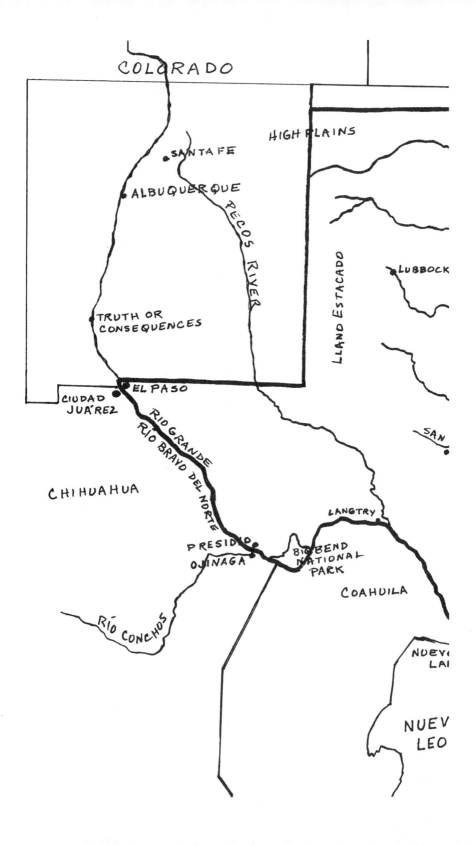

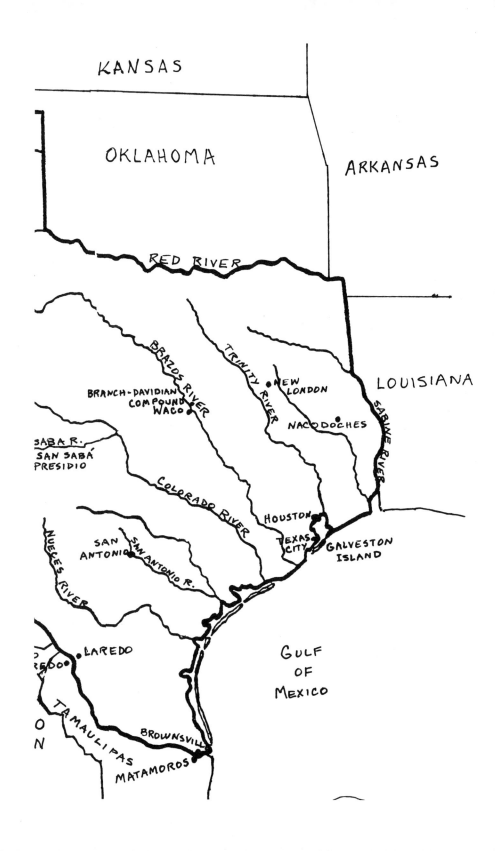

TEXAS DISASTERS

Wind, Flood, and Fire

Mona D. Sizer

A REPUBLIC OF TEXAS PRESS BOOK
TAYLOR TRADE PUBLISHING
Lanham • New York • Dallas • Toronto • Oxford

A Republic of Texas Press Book

Published by Taylor Trade Publishing
An imprint of The Rowman & Littlefield Publishing Group, Inc.
4501 Forbes Boulevard, Suite 200
Lanham, Maryland 20706

Distributed by NATIONAL BOOK NETWORK

Library of Congress Cataloging-in-Publication Data

Sizer, Mona D.
    Texas disasters : wind, flood, and fire / Mona Sizer.
        p.   cm.
    Includes bibliographical references and index.
    ISBN 1-58979-171-1 (pbk. : alk. paper)
    1. Natural disasters—Texas. I. Title.
GB5010.S49 2004
976.4—dc22   2004012467

∞ ™ The paper used in this publication meets the
minimum requirements of American National Standard for
Information Sciences—Permanence of Paper for Printed
Library Materials, ANSI/NISO Z39.48-1992.

Manufactured in the United States of America.

CONTENTS

ACKNOWLEDGMENTS

I'd like to acknowledge my husband, Jim, who has listened attentively to almost every word in this book, including the ballads. What a clever, cogent sounding board he's made. He's also gone with me on some arduous photo shoots for the pictures in the book. At 5 A.M. in the Palo Duro Canyon with ice in the streams and our breath frosting in our faces, he never faltered. What a prince!

Thanks to Ruth and Bob Welch, two of the best friends anyone could have. When I couldn't find the Branch Davidian compound outside Waco, they not only found it, but went back for a second shoot. Their photos constitute an eerie testimony to that haunted place.

Thanks to Janet Harris and Rick Rinehart for approving this work. It's been tougher than I ever imagined to write a book in which I deemed a chapter successful only if it made me weep.

Thanks to Allen Damron for his expert critique of my ballads. I'm blessed to have someone with nearly fifty years of singing and entertaining to approve of my work.

Thanks to all my friends who encouraged me and never reproved me when I said, "I'm writing today."

Thanks to the librarians, archivists, historians, museum directors, guides, photojournalists, and advisors at sites all over Texas who gave me so much cooperation.

Finally, my personal thanks to people who were exceptionally helpful to me in my travels: Les Hassell, photojournalist at the *Longview News-Journal*; Ric Vasquez, photo editor of the *Valley Morning Star*; Mollie Ward, museum director at the London Museum; Beth Steiner at the Moore

Memorial Library in Texas City; the folks at the Texas City Museum; the good people at the Waco–McLennan County Library; the San Antonio Public Library archivist; and the archivist at the Rosenberg Library in Galveston. Thanks also to individuals along the way who directed me, led me, and told me their stories. Texas is a wonderful place to do research.

IN THE MIDST OF LIFE

For most Texans life is a joy. What is not to love about a state with mountains, seashores, woodlands, prairies, deserts, rivers? What is not to love when a person can choose whether to live miles from other human beings or to brush shoulders with hundreds every day? What is not to love about a state with such a rich heritage of many peoples coming together to create a splendid culture?

Part of that culture is the heritage of independence, of courage in the face of death, of heroes who gave the full measure, of empire builders who created opportunities for thousands, of valiant women who led as well as followed, of four presidents. The list goes on and on.

But not all of Texas is joyful or rich. The huge state with many ecosystems and rapidly changing weather patterns has been the scene of many horrendous events. Some happened as the result of bad luck. Some have been deemed acts of God. Some have been investigated and found to be acts of blind stupidity.

Some of these acts man has performed and continues to perform despite red flags waving and sirens wailing. Those hang over his head like the chilled-steel sword of Damocles.

God, nature, and man. A triumvirate for great good fortune and for dreadful mischance. So long as he lives, man will see both sides of the coin. Every day creates a danger somewhere.

Fortunately for Texas, most days are bright.

The ones that are not are disasters.

Hundreds, even thousands, of lives are lost. Property is destroyed without hope of replacement. Treasure is spent with no hope of gaining more. What we love the most is taken from us.

There is nothing left to do except read of these terrible events, while marveling that we are here to do so.

Even with all our technology, with all our support systems, and with all our confidence in the twenty-first century, in the midst of life we are at the mercy of chance, man, and God.

WHY WE SING

Man is a singing animal. He loves the sound of his own voice. He sings as a child, cocking his little head to one side as he listens to a bird and tries to imitate it. He sings to his lover to court her, and he sings to his babes in their cradles. He sings to himself as he works. He sings as he goes marching into battle. He sings to his God. And he sings as he lowers his brothers into their final resting places.

Even before he learned to write, he sang songs. Eventually, he began to write them down and developed a universal language for annotating their tunes. He invented numberless musical instruments to replicate the notes he hears in his mind.

Among his vital subjects are the disasters that rise to haunt his dreams and interrupt the smooth flow of his existence. Perhaps his singing voice releases the emotion in ways that allow him to endure his pain with greater forbearance.

The tragedies described in this book called for a bit more than just their recounting. Please allow me to sing my songs in emotional response to the fates of so many who are gone forever. Bear with me as my ballads commemorate each disaster at the end of each chapter. Each is as chary of detail as the ballads of old. Like them, each one is a song from the heart.

1

HEADING: HOME

In 1976 the National Aeronautics and Space Agency (NASA) set a goal to build a space transportation system (STS) to carry men and machinery to a space platform, unload its cargo, fly back into Earth's orbit, and land safely. It was the most ambitious project America had devised. Riding on the enthusiasm engendered by the *Mercury, Gemini,* and *Apollo* successes with only very minor glitches and spurred by America's love of being first and best in world, Congress voted money to build five STS shuttles and a test vehicle.

Even while *Columbia,* the first of these, was being built, Orbiter Vehicle 101 was constructed. Seeking favorable publicity for the incredibly expensive program and bowing to pressure from science fiction fans, NASA took its name from a popular TV series. Never meant to leave Earth's atmosphere, it was a test ship to check out the aerodynamic stability of the airframe. While all the scientists and engineers held their breath, it was launched into the atmosphere. Its booster rockets dropped away. In 1977 America's first spaceship *Enterprise* flew free, then descended from twenty-four thousand feet to land on the Rogers Dry Lakebed at Edwards Air Force Base.

Eventually, the fleet designed for space flight and return included the tragic *Challenger* and *Columbia.* Today only three remain: *Discovery, Atlantis,* and *Endeavor.*

Photojournalist Les Hassell of the *Longview News-Journal* jerked awake on February 1, 2003, to a series of explosions that rattled the windows and shook the house. Many East Texans, still troubled with nightmares of September 11, 2001, thought America had been attacked a second time. Ordi-

> "When you launch in a rocket, you're not really flying that rocket; you're just hanging on."
>
> **Michael P. Anderson, payload commander**

narily a dead-to-the-world sleeper until noon, Les at first believed, as many people did, that a train had wrecked or a plane had crashed nearby.

Friend and fellow photojournalist Kevin Green called minutes later to tell Les he was heading for Nacogdoches eighty miles away where pieces of *Columbia* were raining down into people's yards, on their farms and ranches, and throughout the area known as the Piney Woods.

Les arrived in Nacogdoches to find that the situation was generally well in hand. It was just like any other "ordinary" disaster. Because of all the tragic acts of God and man in Texas's colorful history, the state's emergency plans are honed sharp as a bowie knife.

Sheriff Tom Maddox of Sabine County heard the sonic boom. He turned to his deputy. "Man, we have got a mess. Call all the hands. I don't know what it is, but whatever it is, it is bad."

Immediately, all his lines lit up. Within fifteen minutes he got a call that the *Columbia* had passed overhead, but no one had heard from it since. Then things began falling in people's yards. "Human remains had been found also. I went out and checked," Maddox reported, "and sure enough it was."

By the time the government agents and the press arrived, the sheriff and the police were maintaining order and dealing efficiently with the media flood that had gridlocked the historic college town.

With the arrival of the National Guard, a search was organized while NASA warned people not to pick up debris. The agency would have preferred to retrieve the entire wreck by itself, except that the field to be searched extended throughout East Texas into Louisiana and Arkansas. Joining in the hunt, twenty thousand volunteers cooperated with authorities, behaving as Texans have behaved in emergency situations throughout the state's history.

A huge search was organized in the largely untouched forest and fields. Many areas were remote, with only the remains of old logging trails through the trees. Rainy weather hampered recovery efforts. Searchers rode horse-

The search begins with the grid of each county in East Texas. Courtesy of Les Hassell, photojournalist, Longview News-Journal.

back, drove all-terrain vehicles, and later manned motorized parachutes to skim the trees two hundred feet above the ground.

Les himself went with one team into the woods and took pictures of small pieces as people came upon them and marked them with yellow flags. Large pieces of the ship were encircled with yellow plastic crime-scene tape.

A man with a camera operates with a sense that the lens is the eye, the entity. He sees through it in terms of light and camera angles. He moves methodically and professionally taking pictures of things that would disturb him mightily if the lens did not psychologically distance him from reality.

In one vivid case, Les felt his detachment deserting him. To this day he remains moved by the memory of his subject. He had focused on the sole of a boot lying on the forest floor on a bed of yellow, orange, and brown leaves. Suddenly, the experience was all too wrenching. That ruined boot suddenly conjured up a vision of an American footprint in the dust of the moon and the American flag beside it.

What Les saw was seven beautiful, brilliant people—surely among the best that this world has produced—disintegrating, burning, falling to Earth in a crash that shook the soul of a nation.

One of them might one day have walked on the moon.

The ruined boot belonging to one of the astronauts. Courtesy of Les Hassell, photojournalist, Longview News-Journal.

On May 5, 1961, five months into John F. Kennedy's sadly abbreviated term of office, Alan Shepherd rode a spacecraft in a suborbital flight that lasted just fifteen minutes. The world was less than impressed. The Russian Yuri Gagarin had made a complete orbit of the Earth and returned safely on April 12.

The United States was embarrassed, its pride damaged. It was accustomed to being first in everything. And so it began a race far, far behind. In a race of these proportions, some things must always be sacrificed in order to win. Such is certainly the case of the American/Russian contest to which China added an astronaut in October 2003. The difference between the American race and others is the public's right to know. When America

"I applied [to NASA] four different times, and interviewed two different times, and then was hired after the second interview."

Rick Husband, mission commander

makes a mistake, the media capture it and send it round the world. When China launched her first astronaut, no one knew of him until the man was safely back on Earth. No one will ever know if previous launches were made and failed, and men died.

Space shuttles have two hundred fifty million parts. With so many pieces to go wrong, the truly amazing thing is that only two space shuttles have crashed out of 113 shuttle flights. Americans need to ask themselves how many planes crashed in the forty-two years after Kitty Hawk. Despite fail-safes and backups, despite system checks and dedicated men, the integrity of every single component is impossible to check. Likewise, pressure comes at every turn to get it right the first time so that the launches can go on as scheduled and the public can have its "reality entertainment."

At the outset the odds of a shuttle going into space and returning seemed impossible. The flights of *Gemini* and *Apollo* were made in disposable spacecraft that fell into the ocean with all their parts lost except the capsule containing the astronauts. The riders were facing backward and simply rode the falling, plasma-covered, shielded capsules into the sea, where they rocked and bobbed until Navy SEALS fastened hooks to their sides to lift them up onto ships. The astronauts climbed out, and the capsules were stripped of their valuable data and shipped off to museums.

In eighteen years of shuttle flights, only one ship had been lost before 2003. The ill-fated *Challenger* with its deteriorated rubber O-rings crashed within seventy-three seconds of takeoff. The feeling was that once the ships got into space everyone could relax. Little could happen on a landing with experienced pilots bringing them in.

The space program has always needed good publicity. The billions of dollars required to run the program are voted on by the American taxpayer, who might quickly tire if the excitement didn't keep building. And the excitement quickly turned to yawns. When *Apollo 13* was in dire distress on its homeward flight, millions of television viewers were unhappy because Walter Cronkite kept interrupting the latest chapter of "Batman."

> "I'll tell you, there's nothing better than listening to a good album and looking out the window and watching the world go by while you pedal on the [exercise] bike."
>
> **William C. McCool, pilot**

Sending up the "teacher in space" Krista McAuliffe, who won a nationwide contest to teach lessons in classrooms from Alaska to Florida, was a publicity stunt to generate interest among younger people and encourage millions to vote for more funding. When *Challenger* exploded on the viewing screens in thousands of American schools, little children wept hysterically. The space program got a severe black eye from which it took a long time to recover.

Absolutely no one in the space program wanted such a disaster to occur again. Still, the feeling was that anyone with nattering concerns should keep his mouth shut.

The 113th shuttle flight was the twenty-eighth flight of the venerable *Columbia*, commissioned April 12, 1981, when Ronald Reagan was president. This workhorse of the fleet had flown more missions than any other vehicle. She had been upgraded and modified three times—the last being in 1999, when the work took far longer than expected. The crews had been announced in 2000, but the ship's overhaul still wasn't completed until 2002. The needs to supply and rotate the crews of the International Space Station kept pushing *Columbia*'s next mission back. Finally, when the flight date was set, cracks were discovered in her engines as well as the engines of two of her sister ships. All had to be repaired.

Then *Columbia* sat on the launch pad for thirty-nine days, more than two weeks longer than usual, while Cape Canaveral received nearly four times the usual amount of rain. The foam insulation around the external fuel tank was drenched. The engineers feared that water soaking into the insulation could turn to ice when the tank was filled with supercold liquid hydrogen and liquid oxygen before the launch. More serious rumors circulated. Was the space program deteriorating? Was *Columbia* really ready to go? Certainly, a troubling chain of events seemed to be binding her to Earth.

Finally, on January 14, 2003, the ground crew began to load the liquid hydrogen and oxygen into the tanks that provided electricity for the spaceship. Food went into lockers on the mid-deck. The experiments were stowed in the cargo bay. The seven who would fly on *Columbia* tried to get a few hours' sleep while she waited for them, gleaming white, bathed in brilliant searchlights on the launch pad.

The hull of the ship itself was constructed of aluminum, a lightweight metal that could not possibly withstand the stresses of takeoff, much less the temperatures of three thousand degrees Fahrenheit and the overwhelming pounds per square inch of drag at reentry. Rather than protect her with steel, which would add overwhelming weight, her skin was covered with thirty thousand foamed-silica tiles. Incredibly lightweight, they dissipated heat so rapidly that a tile could be removed from the oven and held by its edges bare-handed while inside it was still red-hot.

Unfortunately, these tiles were expensive to manufacture and tedious to attach to the shuttle's hull, but with the successful publicity program bringing in a nearly unlimited supply of taxpayer money, NASA paid the price. Every tile had to be shaped in a slightly different manner to adhere to the hull in the precise shape needed for that spot. Each tile had its own number. The documentation required a mountain of paperwork. Likewise, the engineers found the tiles couldn't simply be stuck onto the flexible aluminum skin. Between the tiles and the hull they added a blanket of Nomex felt to act as a buffer and insulator. Nomex, a nylon, flame-resistant, heat-resistant material, is most famously seen on television in the brilliantly colored suits of Indianapolis 500 and NASCAR drivers.

A potential problem was that if even a single tile were pulled off by the friction of launch or reentry, a zipper effect might occur. All the tiles in that particular line would be ripped away, exposing the fragile underskin to temperatures that would destroy the ship and its crew. Despite several attempts, the experts were not able to develop any kind of kit that a crewman could take outside to make a repair while the ship was in orbit.

Given the importance of the nation's getting a boost from a successful flight after the horrors of September 11, 2001, optimism ran high for the best publicity ever. Confidence was in the air. An almost "been there; done that" aura surrounded the people on the ground. No one seemed particularly nervous now that the ship was in position to launch—snug between the solid fuel rocket boosters and against the external fuel tank insulated with foam. The tank and boosters had all been checked for leakage of their frozen fuels and for the possibility of fires. All the insulating foam seemed unaffected by recent rains as well as firmly attached to the gigantic tank.

At 9:11 A.M. the astronauts were all strapped into their seats and the closeout crew had shut the hatch.

At 10:27 A.M. Test Director Jeff Spaulding took a final poll of all the systems. Three minutes later the Ground Launch Sequencer took over. Nine minutes later flame blazed below the main engines. The ground shook for a mile around as *Columbia* thrust slowly upward, then faster. In ninety seconds she had burned so much fuel that she weighed half of what she did at 10:39. Eight and a half minutes later, she was in orbit, flying free around and above Earth, her crew stealing breathtaking looks out the window at the wonders of oceans and continents, mountains and deserts, snowstorms and rainstorms.

Most people round the world probably wonder what astronauts do while they're circling the globe. Do they just sit around perhaps reading paperback novels, looking out the window, turning somersaults in their weightless environment, listening to music, e-mailing home, and occasionally taking a walk in space?

Every minute aboard any shuttle is precious. The tremendous expense involved in putting the crew into space is ever in their minds, along with the determination to do everything required of them and then more—to excel beyond all measure. Once *Columbia*'s crew freed themselves from their launch seats, they fell immediately to work, each in his prearranged team, unloading the stowed items. Then B Team climbed into the sleep supports that keep them stationary in zero gravity for six hours.

The A Team, consisting of Rick Husband, Kalpana Chawla, Laurel Clark, and Israeli astronaut Ilan Ramon, went immediately to work on the Israeli Mediterranean Dust Experiment, which studied mineral dust in the atmosphere over the Mediterranean Sea. During the flight, Ramon sent home the first calibrated images of "elf," an atmospheric electrical halo that glows over the tops of thunderstorms. A week later, he sent images of "sprite," an electrical phenomenon like "elf." It appears over exceptionally

> "We get to participate in fundamental research that will contribute to medical understanding, physical sciences understanding, and a better understanding of the Earth."
>
> **David M. Brown, mission specialist 1**

large thunderstorms and sends electrical discharges into the Earth's upper atmosphere.

Other, separate experiments, suggested by students around the world, involved harvester ants, Australian spiders, Chinese silkworms and their larvae, carpenter bees, developing fish embryos, and thirteen rats. Most of these were conducted not only because of the useful information they might generate, but also because the space program needed to maintain a constant stream of publicity aimed at eager students in the public school science programs, and their parents—the voters. As a matter of record, when the Russians launched Sputnik during Nikita Khrushchev's administration, school science departments came under scrutiny, their share of the school budget got larger, and the annual science project was born.

Other experiments sent data from space extrapolated in procedures impossible to duplicate except in zero gravity. For example, in zero gravity an open flame does not waver. The effects of soot were studied to learn how it created pollution. Laurel Clark, the medical doctor in the crew, monitored an experiment that studied cancerous prostate cells, sending home data that might prove useful in finding a cure for the disease.

Of importance to the space program itself was the data collected as the crew constantly tested their own bodies, drawing blood to record loss of calcium, manufacture of protein, and changes in saliva and urine. The future, as stated by President George W. Bush, now focuses on a mission to Mars, but all sorts of problems must be solved before such a mission can be undertaken. Before a crew can be sent, the problem of physical deterioration in a zero gravity environment has to be conquered. At current shuttle speeds, no one would even be able to move in Mars's gravity by the time

---

"When you talk to these [Holocaust survivors] and you tell them that you are going into space as an Israeli astronaut, they look at you as a dream they could never have dreamed of."

Ilan Ramon, payload specialist

Note: Captain Ilan Ramon was one of eight fighter pilots who flew the Israeli raid to destroy the French nuclear reactor outside Baghdad in June 1981.

he arrived. Much, much more must be learned and much technology must be improved before such a voyage can be manned.

For twenty-four hours a day over fourteen days, the crew took optimum advantage of their precious minutes in space fulfilling their obligations. So much energy and national treasure had been expended to keep them there. Even so their eyes strayed to the infinite world outside their window.

Their final day in space was devoted to chores, in particular tying everything down and stowing it in its proper place. After six hours, they strapped themselves in to wait until Mission Control gave the go-ahead. Two hundred miles above Earth and twenty times the speed of sound, Chawla enjoyed a nostalgic look down at the eternal snows of the Himalayas, the bulwark of her country.

At 7:00 A.M. Eastern Standard Time, the crew locked everything down. An hour and fifteen minutes later they were given approval to land. *Columbia* was then flying backward, although no one on board was physically aware of that fact. In space there is no up or down. Commander Husband and Pilot McCool began the deorbit burn, firing several rockets to slow the speeding craft. The shuttle's computers moved the ship to face forward for landing.

At 8:45 A.M. *Columbia* pierced the outer fringes of Earth's atmosphere north of Hawaii, where it was still the middle of the night. Those who looked up saw at four hundred thousand feet a glowing pink comet streaking across the sky in sweeping S-turns. On board, McCool and Husband were slowing the spacecraft while carefully monitoring the dials and indicators that recorded course, deceleration, temperature, and hydraulics.

The pink glow was the heat surrounding the more than thirty thousand protective ceramic tiles that covered her aluminum skin. As friction from the entry mounted, the pink turned red, then searing white. The ship was riding nose forward in the plasma shield made up of a buffer of superheated gases. Within this shield, communication with Mission Control was impossible.

"Whenever I get to look out [of *Columbia*], it's glorious. Even the stars have a special brightness."

Laurel Clark, mission specialist 4

Only a few minutes remained. In less than half an hour, they would touch down in front of their families and friends in the viewing stands, NASA officials, various bigwigs, and, of course, the all-important press corps.

At 8:53, as *Columbia* roared over San Francisco where people were still not awake, various monitors indicated a halt in the flow of information regarding the temperature of the hydraulic systems in the ship's left wing. The anomaly was so slight, it was deemed nothing to worry about. Tiny glitches frequently occurred. Mission Control didn't even notify the crew.

Three minutes later, over Utah, the left landing gear and brake lining showed a temperature spike of sixty degrees. Mission Control sat up alertly. What the hell happened? Two minutes later, in the skin on the left side of the ship, the temperature sensors went dead.

Those lights winking out created absolute mayhem at Mission Control. People jumped to their feet, tapped at their keyboards, stared at their screens.

Against all odds, the ship was in big trouble.

As *Columbia* streaked across the Texas panhandle, Spacecraft Communicator Charlie Hobaugh radioed the crew, "*Columbia,* Houston. We see your tire-pressure message."

Commander Husband replied, "Roger. Buh . . ."

To Hobaugh's horror and the horror of all the seasoned veterans at Mission Control, voice communications went completely dead. Someone or something had literally pulled the plug. Every form of communication from the ship's hundreds of systems, the constant stream of telemetry, including the monitors on the crew, ceased.

Hobaugh tried again. "*Columbia,* Houston. Com check."

There was nothing but static where the open line had been.

"*Columbia,* Houston. UHF com check."

Nothing. Absolutely nothing but static.

Again Hobaugh called. And again and again.

Only rookies in Mission Control remained hopeful that only a minor electrical glitch had occurred. The ship was only sixteen minutes from touchdown for God's sake. It was back in Earth's atmosphere, coming home. Only fourteen hundred miles from destination. All they had to do was glide in. Surely they could just glide in?

The senior members of Mission Control knew much worse had happened. They also knew that no "gliding in" was possible through the friction of Earth's atmosphere.

Columbia was dead.

All across Texas, amateur and professional videographers had been tracking the loss for almost the whole distance. Indeed, the disaster that struck *Columbia* could be said to be the most viewed disaster in the history of the world. In the brilliant blue and cloudless sky of a Texas dawn, debris began to break away from the ship that millions knew was coming in for a landing.

Each piece of debris falling behind her left a flaming trail, a multitude of comets signaling disappointment, destruction, and death. Thousands upon thousands of savvy Texans watched with growing concern. They looked up on their way out to pick up their papers. They stared up through their windshields on their way to work. They paused as they walked their dogs. They gazed open-mouthed as they waited at bus stops.

In dawning horror they watched burning corpses streaking by above their heads, incinerating in the pristine atmosphere as the workhorse of the Space Transportation System, the perfectly engineered spaceship loaded with a priceless crew and valuable equipment, shattered and fell to Earth.

It was the *Titanic* of the skies.

At the Kennedy Space Center in Florida, all the families waited. As the scheduled landing time approached, they began a countdown from ten to zero, waiting for the shuttle to appear. But when the sonic booms did not come, when no sleek white ship appeared, everyone became very quiet. Everyone except the very youngest children knew exactly what had happened.

The silence grew. As the minutes passed, everyone knew there was no one to wait for.

The people of East Texas heard the sonic booms. Some of those already outside or those who ran outside in their night clothes saw horrific sights. From Palestine, Texas, to Louisiana and Arkansas, a five-hundred-square-mile swath of rural America's forests, pastures, and fertile farmland, was stip-

"[Being accepted into the space program] is almost like having won the lottery or something."

Kalpana Chawla, mission specialist 2

pled with smoking, crumpled metal. Miraculously, no one was struck or even injured.

A man fishing in Toledo Bend Reservoir on the Texas–Louisiana border heard a piece "fluttering" down above him. When he looked around, he saw a chunk of metal easily the size of a compact car slam into the water with a horrendous splash. From his report NASA investigators were able to use sonar to locate and retrieve it.

In Hemphill on the western edge of the Sabine National Forest, the shuttle's nosecone was discovered relatively intact. It had sustained little damage from the intense heat of reentry. In another location a seven-

The rugged terrain of East Texas frustrates the searchers. Courtesy of Les Hassell, photojournalist, Longview News-Journal.

hundred-pound rocket engine punched a twelve-foot hole in the ground and threw dirt thirty-five feet in the air.

Hundreds of smoldering chunks of twisted metal struck Nacogdoches. In his front yard, one man found a nine-inch-long, two-inch-wide piece of melted metal with heat burns. In San Augustine a few miles east, people covered their faces at the sight of charred body parts.

NASA officials warned citizens not to touch anything they found. Four extremely toxic compounds—raw hydrazine, monomethyl hydrazine, nitrogen tetroxide, and pure ammonia—were used as fuel and coolant aboard every shuttle. The silica fibers from the heat-resistant tiles could cause lung damage, and seemingly innocent pieces of metal might be pyrotechnical devices such as explosive bolts. Despite all the warnings, many good citizens simply picked up the pieces they found in their yards and brought them to the proper authorities.

In the final count twenty-two thousand responders from 130 government agencies, volunteer agencies, private groups, and contractors answered the call. More than eighty thousand pieces were retrieved over a two-state area. Still, only about 40 percent of the eighty-four-thousand-pound shuttle was recovered. The deep woods, lakes, and bayous around the Sabine River hold their secrets forever.

What has not been discovered as of this writing is a top-secret device that communicated encrypted messages between the shuttle and Mission Control. Searchers were not given so much as a picture of the entire device, only of the faceplate, which read "Secret Government Property."

At length NASA officials at Cape Canaveral with only minimal plans for study collected all the twisted, charred, smashed pieces on the floor of a hangar at the Kennedy Space Center. In July 2003 the Smithsonian National Air and Space Museum expressed interest in keeping some pieces. They stated firmly that they did not plan to display any of them in the near future because of "the ghoulish factor." At the time of this writing, no decisions have been made.

Because of the unblinking eye of universal press coverage, the whole world was involved in the disaster. Condolences poured in. Grief was especially sharp in Israel and in India. The European Space Agency called the loss "a devastating event in the history of space."

At NASA and in the U.S. Congress, the search for answers began. How had a seemingly perfect mission ended so tragically? Could the whole disaster have been averted? Who or what was to blame?

For those hardcore space buffs in the Congress, the disaster was tragic,

Large piece of Columbia *carefully wrapped in plastic and cordoned off by crime-scene tape. Courtesy Les Hassell, photojournalist,* Longview News-Journal.

but they would continue to support the program. From those who saw NASA as a gigantic waste of money, the cost-versus-benefits screams began.

Of immediate concern were the problems in the construction and maintenance of the International Space Station. While the station received supplies from Russian unmanned supply vehicles, American shuttles were the weightlifters that moved people as well as large components. When *Columbia* crashed, 25 percent of the American fleet crashed with her. In March the two American astronauts and the Russian cosmonaut aboard the station were scheduled to return to Earth and be replaced by a fresh crew. Somewhere down the line, some shuttle was going to have to double up.

While NASA shuddered at the prospect of a March launch before they could complete a thorough investigation, they knew it could not be delayed for long. Already a leak in an interior line had been detected aboard the station. Those who sought to end the program were confounded. America had already promised maintenance of the space station to Russia and to the world. Russia could not handle it alone. The imperative was to find some answers—quickly.

"One thing we're not going to do, which was done with *Challenger,* is lock it up and bury it and pretend that it didn't happen," NASA administrator Sean O'Keefe promised. He called for two investigating boards: one within the space agency and one outside consisting of five military men, the chief of the Aviation Safety Division for the Transportation Department, and the director of the Federal Aviation Administration. NASA also requested help from the National Transportation Safety Board at Barksdale Air Force Base outside Shreveport, Louisiana, just north of the crash site. Meanwhile, the House Science Committee announced its own investigation.

It found plenty to investigate. Within hours all flight data recorded since the launch was impounded, including the hundreds of telemetry readings. All the private companies, including Boeing and Lockheed Martin, which make up the United Space Alliance, involved in the construction and maintenance of the shuttles came under scrutiny.

Although terrorists were mentioned first, they were quickly ruled out. *Columbia* was traveling far too fast and high for any known weapon to come near it. A bomb somehow placed aboard was even less likely. Tourists were no longer allowed near a shuttle on the launch pad. Liftoff times were a guarded secret until twenty-four hours before launch. The confines of the shuttle precluded any sort of device being hidden away. Every square inch of available space was inspected many times. Nothing could have been smuggled aboard.

Almost immediately the investigative teams looked at the liftoff. If the problem had developed then, the *Columbia* and her crew had flown for sixteen days unaware of any problems. The press speculated endlessly about that possibility. The idea of a doomed ship and a doomed crew cruising happily around Earth oblivious of their fate upset people nationwide.

Investigative boards took a long, hard look at a two-foot-long chunk of foam insulation from the external fuel tank. During liftoff it had been photographed striking the shuttle's left wing. Shuttle Program Manager Ron Dittemore quickly discounted that strike as the culprit. The foam was lightweight. Pieces of it had flaked off before and had caused no damage in other flights.

"There are a lot of things in this business that look like the smoking gun but that turn out not even to be close," Dittemore declared. He theorized that a missing tile in *Columbia*'s protective skin had created the dreaded zipper effect, stripping the ship down to her aluminum skin, which then melted to create the breach.

Another possibility was that one of the two-foot-long, forty-pound bolts that connected the solid-rocket boosters to the external fuel tank had broken off on liftoff and smashed against the left wing. The result would have been catastrophic. But there was no proof that a bolt had broken.

Before the cause was discovered, the questions were already coming hard and fast, aimed directly at the Mission Control crews and the men in charge of NASA themselves. Could *Columbia*'s crew have been saved? What could have been done to bring them home? When NASA stammered and appeared to close ranks, accusations of a "NASA culture" arose. Congress questioned people in lower echelons, where they discovered many problems.

New hands in NASA reported being instructed to table safety concerns rather than allow them to delay launches. Top priority was given to minor experiments elicited from school children involving ants, bees, and rats. Flights were to be made on schedule in the interest of good publicity and television coverage as much as for the information garnered.

As ever, the generals weren't listening to the men in the trenches. In fact, the *Wall Street Journal* reported that NASA had done "little since the 1986 explosion of the space shuttle *Challenger* to foster an environment in which safety concerns flowed freely from low-level engineers to top NASA managers." Spending cuts and mounting pressures to complete the International Space Station had shifted the emphasis to schedules rather than safety. Painting a rosy picture for the press and the voters was paramount.

While all the concerns lay in getting the flights up into space, very little thought had ever been given to getting them home. In retrospect NASA's failure to arrange for rescue seems criminally negligent. It harkens back to World War I, when British pilots were not issued parachutes because the new devices were deemed bad for morale. NASA seemed to have been concerned less with morale and more with the public's perception of shuttle flights as safe. Because no arrangements had been made, even if the damage had been noted during the flight, nothing could have been done. Many came to realize that if an emergency or contingency shuttle could have been ready to go with a docking device, the personnel could have been transferred. The result would have been a heroic rescue and great publicity.

On February 19, 2004, an announcement was made that a second shuttle would be ready to go to the space station to retrieve any shuttle crew that might have to "ditch" in space. The launch to go to the shuttle was slated for March or April.

Meanwhile, the various boards scrutinized all the data to discover what had caused the accident. Four months later they found their smoking gun.

Despite Ron Dittemore's downplay of the insulating foam, tests were scheduled.

Columbia Accident Investigation Board member Scott Hubbard performed a test on a wing from *Columbia*'s sister ship *Atlantis*. About a hundred observers gathered in a field in San Antonio on Monday, July 8. A 1.67-pound chunk of foam insulation was loaded into a thirty-five-foot nitrogen-pressurized gun to simulate a force of 530-miles-per-hour—the force with which the shuttle rose.

The innocuous foam, scarcely bigger than a couple of pounds of hamburger, blew a gaping sixteen-inch hole in the carbon-reinforced panel. Sixteen high-speed cameras captured the impact. Hundreds of sensors had been attached to the wing. Some of their gauges were damaged.

"It was in here," *Columbia* Accident Investigation Board member Scott Hubbard reported, smacking his fist into his belly. "It was a visceral reaction. It was shortly followed by 'Oh, my God.'" He concluded that without question the damage was of the kind that most certainly would have brought down the shuttle.

Columbia's crew would have felt nothing in their roaring, rumbling, vibrating ride. Further investigation of the wing concluded that any repairs mid-flight would have been impossible.

Later, more tests were performed. All duplicated the damage of the first test. A full year after the disaster, NASA determined that either air or liquefied nitrogen had seeped into a crack or void in the foam. The trapped material had expanded as the shuttle rose and had blown off a chunk of foam the size of a suitcase. *Columbia*'s wing had been destroyed. The crew had been riding a death ship with no way to get home.

The initial shocking revelation was followed within twenty-four hours by the discovery of images in NASA's records and procured by the Associated Press under the Freedom of Information Act. The pictures showed heat damage caused by a small leak through a seam in *Atlantis*'s left wing, which was breached in May 2000 on its way home from the space station. Superheated gases had scorched components inside the spacecraft. NASA had quietly ordered the leak repaired, buried the data, and sent *Atlantis* into space again in four months. None of the astronauts was told about any problems.

Clearly, NASA had abdicated much of its responsibility for the safety of manned space flight. Boeing and Lockheed Martin had the contracts in their hands. They had acted in the interest of profits. Further assessment by the *Columbia* Accident Investigation Board revealed that NASA's analysis of the foam's capability had been determined by an outdated software program

Boeing had furnished to a team of largely inexperienced engineers. The program, of course, found nothing to require an expensive remedy.

In the wake of the board's findings, NASA, Boeing, and Lockheed Martin are working on a new software-analysis tool and looking for ways to insulate the fuel tanks without using the foam at all.

Tragically, their efforts come too late. Despite the president's call for a new initiative, Congress and the voters are now asking the questions dreaded by NASA and the independent contractors to whom 85 percent of the budget goes. Is this program irreparably flawed? Can we go no farther into space? For now, managers are gambling, playing too close to too many margins, and ignoring too many little pieces of risk.

When the dice roll snake eyes, a disaster of monumental proportions is the result. It could happen again.

The shuttle had been doomed after only eighty-three seconds in flight, even before the external fuel tank had fallen away. Unlike the *Challenger,* *Columbia* had managed to fly on into space and complete her mission. Her problem occurred when she could not bring her people home.

In December 2003 the Space Center in Houston announced, "NASA plans to embed high-tech sensors in the wings of the three remaining space shuttles to detect any blows from debris." As of this writing, the sensors will only determine whether debris hit the wing, not the degree of damage. If the sensors detect a hit, follow-up will consist of on-site inspection from a boom with cameras and lasers while the shuttle is orbiting.

Still missing from this pitiful installation is computer software needed to operate the boom. More important, no repair kit has yet been developed for the carbon panels where the debris would most likely hit. How gruesome to think that the sensors would operate as the shuttle soared into space, and the crew would know they had been hit, but would be unable to determine how serious the strike was. Perhaps by the time the shuttle is launched in 2004, the agency will actually be able to see the damage, but still be unable to make repairs. We can only hope that technology will be there for the crew when they need it.

Beyond the shuttles, most experts agree that Earth's space progress is at a standstill until we develop technology to establish centrifugal gravity within the spaceship. Zero gravity is very bad for us. The bodies of the Russians who set the endurance records in space have never fully recovered. Not only John Glenn, flying at age seventy-seven in *Discovery,* but also all the younger astronauts who return from their tours aboard the space station have to be taken off on stretchers. Their bones are too decalcified and their muscles too atrophied to carry them upright. A trip to Mars would require six months going and six months returning. No one staying six months in space has been able to walk for weeks afterward.

So far, no NASA engineers in the upper echelons have tried any innovations to provide centrifugal gravity in space. They have not even experimented. The spirit of the status quo has replaced the spirit of adventure and discovery that once animated NASA.

Like a ghost from a brighter, more innovative time, The *Enterprise,* the test ship for the space shuttle program, flew again on December 5, 2003. From the hangar where she had gathered dust for a quarter of century, she took off for a short flight to the new Smithsonian National Air and Space Museum Steven F. Udvar-Hazy Center, the giant hangar for the historic, obsolete ships of the past. Located in Chantilly, Virginia, it is only a few miles outside of Washington, D.C., near Dulles International Airport. There with the *Enola Gay* and the *Spirit of St. Louis,* she will satisfy the curiosity of tourists.

Is this a prophecy for the shuttle program itself?

It seemed appropriate to this author to let Homer Hickam have the last word. The story of Hickam's youth as the son of a coal miner was recorded in his autobiographical *Rocket Boys* and seen in the biographical movie *October Sky.* As a twenty-year veteran of NASA, a veteran of Viet Nam, and a man of inspiring eloquence, he wrote an article for the *Wall Street Journal* just three months after *Columbia* exploded.

> We can't just shut the thing down. *Atlantis, Discovery,* and *Endeavor* must complete the mission to build the space station. Put tough engineers in charge. Change the launch configuration to move the ships out of the midst of all that noise, vibration, and confusion in the midst of the propellant tank and the two rocket boosters. Fly the mission ten more times over the next four years with hand-picked crews to fulfill our international obligations. Letting the Russians and now the Chinese dominate space is the alternative. America has flown too far and with too much courage for such a dismal and conceivably dangerous outcome.

Only when the space station is completed should the shuttle program be closed as were *Mercury, Gemini,* and *Apollo.* His idea for the next step:

> Replace [the shuttle] . . . with expendable launchers and a shiny new spaceplane.
> And this time put it on top.

"The Seekers"
(To the tune of "Come to the Bower" sung at San Jacinto)

We've trekked through the white snows of Everest,
We've sounded the Pacific's blue deep,
We've tunneled a thousand miles and more
For treasure within our earth's keep.

Silver planes cross our heavens like fireflies.
Our flag's on our moon's desert face.
Joining hands with our fiercest of enemies,
We've set up a station in space.

We know we're too fragile to go there,
But our rovers are rolling on Mars,
While our telescope's sighting the next plateau.
God helps us. We're bound for the stars.

And some of us fall from the heavens,
And some of us drown in the deep.
There's blood on the stones from our tunnels.
Our records their memories we keep.

Restless spirits within ever seeking
The unknown as if it were lost.
Fierce light burns within us eternal.
We can't stop no matter the cost.

No sacrifice strikes us too deeply,
Though our bodies are marked by deep scars.
They're all in the cost of our journey.
God helps us. We're bound for the stars.

2

COMANCHE SUNSET:
THE PLAGUES OF 1849

In 1705 a ragged tribe of bandy-legged Indians straggled down from the Rocky Mountains in present-day Wyoming and wandered into New Mexico. Of all the tribes in the western United States, they were the shortest in stature, the stockiest, and the least respected. Primitive fruit-and-berry pickers, in appearance like Neanderthals from the vanished Stone Age, they encountered the flourishing civilization at the edge of the Spanish Empire. There they begged for some horses from the Spaniards, who had been colonizing the area around Santa Fe since Coronado's expedition of 1540.

The descendants of the tall, light-skinned conquistadors contemptuously refused to part with a single animal. But they always needed grooms and herdsmen. No one knows whether these Indians actually took those menial jobs or whether they simply hung around like stray dogs. Whatever the strategy, they watched closely, and then refused to take no for an answer. One day they stole an entire horse herd and thundered away, no doubt whooping and shrieking.

After their daring act of thievery, they set about becoming what they had always believed themselves to be—the Human Beings. "Human" was the superior designation. All other living things were simply "beings." The deer, the buffalo, the eagle, the hare, the Apache, the Spaniard were all beneath them. Until their theft of the horse herd, their conceit was pathetic. Their designation on the plains was a backward wiggling movement of the index finger. They were the lowly Snake People. But after their mastery of their animals, the Spaniards treated them with respect and called them by their real name—*Komantcia*—Comanche.

The frontier artist George Catlin, who encountered them in 1826, described them as "one of the most unattractive and slovenly-looking races of Indians I have ever seen, but the moment they mount their horses, they seem at once metamorphosed, and surprise the spectator with the ease and grace of their movements."

No historian of any stature believes that the horses that "escaped" from Coronado's expedition were the foundation herds of the American West. The Spaniards were excellent horsemen who cared for their transportation as carefully as NASCAR drivers care for their cars. The horses of the frontier were rustled in herds by the Comanche. Those herds became their destiny, linking them forever with the animal, which was already proving to be the most significant Spanish import to America.

The Comanche became the people on horseback. Man, woman, and child mounted and adapted themselves to a new culture. The horse gave them the power to hunt the buffalo, which in turn became the staple of their lives. Horses on which to hunt the buffalo became wealth. On these a man based his consequence—how many wives he could take, how well he could provide for his family, his status in the tribe. Horse dowries and horse inheritance were still problems of the culture when the Comanche as a people were almost exterminated.

For their horses they adopted and improved the Spanish saddle, the Spanish bit, the Spanish bridle. They added their own efficiently deadly invention, the thong, which the warrior slipped over his head and under his shoulder, attached to his saddle, or simply braided into his horse's mane. With one leg thrown across his mount's back and both his arms free, a warrior could drop over the side of his horse while thundering in a circling charge and shoot a bow or a long gun from under the horse's neck while concealed and protected by the big body.

If the mount was shot, the warrior crawled away and got another. The people who considered themselves superior to all other beings did not love their horses and romanticize them the way the later American cowboy did. The horse was transportation, and through their thievery the Human Beings could get many, many more.

The horse gave them freedom to become completely nomadic like the Mongol tribes. Yet the buffalo gave them a decided advantage over the Asians. The steppes did not have the millions of nomadic animals in herds that stretched to the horizon, placidly moving south in the winter and north in the summer. Buffalo flesh was the Comanche's protein; buffalo hides served as their clothing and, fastened to their horse-drawn travois, as their shelter. The bones created their utensils. Buffalo chips provided their fire. To the physical freedom provided by the horse was added the economic freedom provided by the buffalo.

Eventually, the Comanche formed seven great tribes united by custom and a common language, Uto-Aztekan, which clearly aligned them with the preconquest empire builders of Central Mexico. Like them, the Honey-Eaters, Wanderers, Wasps, Liver-Eaters, Buffalo-Eaters, Yap-Eaters, and Antelopes created an empire of sorts over which they rode at will. The Comanche never plowed a furrow or planted a seed. They followed the buffalo and lived on the backs of their horses.

Unfortunately, a life on horseback created a great problem for Comanche women. Miscarriages were many. A woman could not expect to carry more than one or two children to full term. Therefore, a warrior would ensure his posterity by taking two or three wives. He could certainly provide for them while an unlimited food supply grazed placidly on the horizon.

Following the herds, the Comanche moved onto the Llano Estacado, so called because Coronado had staked it with buffalo bones to mark his way back from searching for the Seven Cities of Gold. There they forced the Spaniards to retreat into their towns and settlements.

Armed with their favorite weapon, the Plains-style lance, and protected by buffalo-hide shields that could turn a musket ball, the Comanche rode to war. At a gallop they would ride two or even three hundred miles deep into their enemy's territory. They struck by the light of the moon, rustled all the horses, but generally ignored or killed the cattle. They killed the men who opposed them, captured prisoners—women and children in particular—and galloped back across the prairies. The women they ransomed or enslaved. The children they adopted into the tribe because their own birthrate was so low.

As their numbers and their raiding increased, the Spaniards took notice. They were determined to extend their dominance by establishing forts farther north. In April 1757 Colonel Diego Ortiz de Parilla led a company of soldiers and five priests north to the San Sabá River. The company built a mission with a palisade a few miles distant from a presidio, or fort. The priests were there to convert the Apaches. The soldiers came to investigate the persistent rumor that a rich lode of silver might be mined in the area. Rumors further promised a fabulous rarity—gold and silver found together.

In March 1758 in the midst of a glorious green spring on the plains, the Comanche moon waxed huge in the sky. Suddenly, in one night all the Apaches around San Sabá disappeared—simply vanished. The next morning, shrieking and shouting, a group of horsemen swooped down to rustle sixty horses from the horse pasture.

Colonel Parilla ordered all the priests to come to the presidio, but they refused to leave the mission. They could not do God's work inside a fort, they maintained. They pointed out the walls of the palisade as an added protection. Parilla shrugged and left them to their prayers with seventeen soldiers to protect them. The next morning as the padres were beginning the mass, an attack began. Parilla's soldiers rushed to the walls to behold two thousand Comanche mounted on horseback, deploying slowly around the palisade.

Padre Terreros, the senior cleric, refused to give the order to fire. Whether he believed that they would not attack or whether he was simply struck speechless with terror will never be known. Certainly, he had never seen anything like the Comanche painted ominous black and red. On their heads they wore buffalo horns, deer antlers, and eagle feathers. All were

Commemorative stone to mark Presidio San Sabá established 1757. Author photo.

armed with lances and bows. In addition, at least a hundred carried French-made muskets, which the soldiers pointed out to the stupefied padres.

In the face of the truly frightening spectacle, Padre Terreros hesitated. A Comanche warrior simply walked up to the gate and pushed it open. The Indians poured into the compound. The padres who tried to trade with them and offer tobacco and beads were ignored. The Comanche chief demanded that Terreros send a message to the presidio.

Within an hour Parilla had sent a detachment from the presidio into an obvious trap. In one Comanche charge the men were all slaughtered, except one who crawled away badly wounded. Back at the mission, the soldiers within the palisade were killed as well. Padre Terreros was gunned down. Then the Comanche began looting the storerooms. Terreros's subordinate, Padre Molina, hid with a few others in the church, which was made of green wood that did not burn. There they survived, gasping in the blinding smoke and praying until the Comanche rode away back across the limitless prairies.

Although a punitive expedition under the command of Colonel Parilla was mounted in August of 1759, it was a disaster. The colonel and his six hundred men, less than half of whom were Spanish troops, met the Coman-

Ruins of the Presidio San Sabá today. Author photo.

che, Wichita, and several other Plains tribes on the banks of the Red River. Parilla maintained that he was defeated by six thousand warriors flying a French flag.

The story of the French flag was probably just a story as was the number of the enemy that just happened to outnumber the troop ten to one. Parilla fought his way out with remarkably small losses considering the size of the force. Unfortunately, he was forced to abandon a trainload of supplies and two cannon he had brought for the purpose of intimidating his enemy.

The Comanche delivered the worst military defeat of Spanish Texas. While the loss of life was small, the psychological defeat was much worse. It was the beginning of the end, for it convinced Spaniards in Mexico City that they could not mount an effective campaign from such a distance.

All Spaniards withdrew to the San Antonio River, where they regrouped their forces. In 1793 the Pueblo de San Carlos del Alamo de Parras secularized the mission San Antonio de Valero on the banks of the San Antonio River. There they built a new presidio, a combination fort, barracks, chapel, and armory, the pride of the Spanish state of Coahuila y Tejas. Indeed, it was the only significant military post between the Rio Grande and the Sabine River. Called familiarly the Alamo, it would figure prominently in Texas history in the nineteenth century.

The settlers of New Spain ranched successfully in that area for over a hundred years, although the population was very small, with only about a thousand soldiers to protect them. Always they were subjected to raids by the powerful Comanche, whose numbers grew "to the numbers of the blades of grass on the prairies."

It was the Comanche's time of glory. They made treaties with the Anglo-Texans moving into the areas—the Old Three Hundred of Stephen F. Austin's colony, the Irish settlers around San Patricio, the German settlers around Fredericksburg. They were indeed the lords of the South Plains by virtue of their totally self-sufficient way of life. They had become the greatest horsemen on this or, arguably, any other continent.

Their battle strategy of fight and flee, as well as their division into a loose confederation, protected them from direct attack by the Spaniards, who had other, more pressing problems from the filibustering French and Americans who were crossing the Sabine in larger numbers. The Spaniards called for settlers who would swear allegiance to the king. Many gave lip service to come across the river.

Meanwhile, with Napoleon on the rampage in Europe, Mexico itself sought to escape from the bonds of Spanish rule. The people found their spiritual leader in Padre Miguel Hidalgo y Costilla, who on September 16, 1810, today a Mexican national holiday, issued the *Grito de Dolores,* his exhortation to overthrow the bad government.

For ten years the revolution raged, while the Comanche were more or less forgotten. During this decade, however, they had their second encounter with smallpox. Their first had been in 1781, but because they were nomadic, its spread was restricted—although it killed almost everyone among them who encountered it.

Smallpox is an ancient disease that probably originated in China and India at least three thousand years ago. It did not reach Europe until the sixth century. The most common form was greatly feared among all populations that encountered it because it was so highly contagious for so long a period.

The onset was twelve days to two weeks after infection either by contact or by inhalation of droplets in the air around the sick person. Within two weeks, the caretaker was likely to develop a high fever also. He ached so severely that he could no longer function. Bedridden, he would develop a rash that quickly spread to his extremities. From that rash, the pox— painful, disfiguring pustules—appeared. So long as the pox scabies clung to the skin of the face, hands and arms, and feet and legs, the disease was spread by human contact.

As with modern plagues, such as AIDS, the largest segment of the victims, those most susceptible, die quickly. A smaller number of victims prove genetically resistant and take longer to die or survive in a debilitated state. A very few never contract it. They are presumed to be genetically immune. Those that are genetically immune are left to mate with the resistant survivors. In this manner, over a thousand years almost any disease becomes racially survivable.

In 1519 when Cortés and his three hundred men attempted an unsuccessful assault on Tenochtitlan near Mexico City, one of his crew had contracted smallpox on a visit to Africa just before the expedition had sailed. That man was captured and held as a hostage. Cortés and his troops fled back to the coast. Since he had already burned his boats, he expected to fight to the death at the village he had named Vera Cruz (True Cross).

No force of Aztecs came after them.

After several months Cortés sent spies to the capital. They returned excitedly with reports of widespread smallpox. The "conqueror" returned with his men and seized the city. Within the next few years, the Aztecs, who had been perhaps twenty million strong, were reduced to thousands. Only those few with natural immunity escaped the disease.

In effect, most of the Indians in Mexico were infected in some way. Those who sought to escape fled into the countryside carrying their contagion with them. Psychologically, the native Americans were devastated as well. Their superstitious beliefs led them to conclude that the strange invaders mounted on a mere seventeen unknown animals—the horses—were employing supernatural powers.

The opposite of H. G. Wells's *War of the Worlds* occurred. Instead of invaders being destroyed by the diseases they encountered, they brought their plagues with them and the diseases conquered for them. The destruction was threefold. First, the numbers of the native armies were so reduced by the disease that they had no power to resist. Second, the deaths of the leaders, who were in some cases among the first to die, created chaos among the survivors. And third, the Spaniards stepped into the midst of the chaos and shrewdly played one faction against another.

Other tribes across North America met the same fate. The Indians of New England and the Great Lakes—the Huron, the Iroquois, and the Mohicans—were reduced to hundreds and unable to offer resistance to the English. Historians disagree as to the total population of the New World at the time of contact with the Europeans. Twenty to thirty million is the most conservative estimate. By the end of the nineteenth century, credible estimates put the surviving populations at just over a million.

The tribes of the New World did not have a millennium in which to survive. Within a century they were almost gone.

To this day there is no cure for smallpox, nor any treatment. Only preventive vaccination eradicated it from the human population in the twentieth century.

At the beginning of the nineteenth century, the revolution in Mexico seemed endless. In Texas, Americans crossed the Sabine and carved out land for themselves while Mexico tore herself apart. In most cases the encroachers simply took over the fertile farmlands of the Cherokee, the Hasinai, the Nacogdoches, and the Nachitoches and moved the Indians off to Oklahoma. Probably the Comanche were aware of what was happening to the tribes east of the Llano since they were in contact with the Wichita, the Tonkawa, and the Waco, whose lands extended into that area.

Whatever the reason, their raids extended deeper and deeper into central Texas, even as far as the Gulf Coast. Another bout with smallpox in

1819 reduced their numbers and inspired them to raid more vigorously for captives and horses. But the people they raided were no longer the padres and their converts and soldiers who had little reason to stay and fight.

Instead, they faced a new breed of frontiersman, the Texan, who had brought his family with him. He had come to put down roots, something the Comanche would never do. Secure in their own arrogance, they considered the Texan farms and ranches suitable for rustling and raiding. The Texans considered the Comanche vermin to be exterminated.

Then a third party entered the war. The Mexicans, under their new dictator General Antonio López de Santa Anna, invaded Texas. For two months he piled up victories at Alamo and Goliad, where he ruthlessly murdered every defender. With the greatest army on the North American continent, he marched eastward, burning and destroying as he went.

April 21, 1836, General Sam Houston gathered the remnants of his army on the plain of San Jacinto. With the Buffalo Bayou at his back and the pitiful Lynchburg ferry his only means of escape, Houston counterattacked. The Mexican army was caught napping, and Santa Anna, the dictator, was captured.

The Comanche had no idea that their way of life and their very people had been eclipsed with that single unbelievable victory. Although Sam Houston wanted to establish a country for the Indians, in particular his friends the Cherokees, he was forced to abandon his hopes within a very few years.

On May 19, 1836, just under a month from the day of San Jacinto, the fort of Elder John Parker, a hard-shell Baptist, with his clan of brothers, cousins, sons, and their wives and children, was attacked. The Comanche had ridden far out of Comanchería to make this raid. They rode up to the gate showing a dirty white flag and asked for water and beef. The parley ended when Elder John Parker said he had no beef to give them. His sons, who had gone back outside to carry his message, were killed in a melee at the gate. The Comanche forced their way in, killed and scalped Parker, stripped his wife, Granny, and staked her to the ground with a lance. They raped her repeatedly. The wives of the other men were attacked as well. Two later died. The Parker men who were still in the fields came running, firing their guns. The Comanche escaped, taking with them five captives: two women, an infant son, and Parker's grandchildren, John and Cynthia Ann.

Granny Parker pulled the lance from her own side and managed to live—her ordeal an embodiment of all that was cruel and barbaric about the

Comanche. The atrocity, so hideous, cried for vengeance. The captive Parker children were the objects of a manhunt. And their tragedy, particularly that of Cynthia Ann, underscored what Texans believed: The only good Indian was a dead Indian. Although Houston tried to reach some equitable solution for his friends the Cherokee, as well as for other peaceful tribes, he had no success during his administration as first president of Texas.

Then he was succeeded by Mirabeau B. Lamar, whose policies and prejudices set the pattern for treatment of the Indians. In his inaugural speech Lamar said,

> The white man and the red man cannot dwell in harmony together. Nature forbids it. I experience no difficulty in deciding . . . to push a rigorous war against them. They shall be made to feel that flight from our borders without hope of return, is preferable.

The destruction and expulsion of the Cherokees from Texas followed within a year.

Although Lamar was wrong about the Cherokee, he was right about the Comanche. They could not live peaceably in the world the Texans were determined to create. Lamar initiated a policy that the U.S. government adopted thirty years later. All Indians must be pursued. Their sanctuaries must be destroyed. Otherwise, the raids they took such pleasure in would continue. Texans came to believe incontrovertibly that if the Indians survived as Indians, they must be rendered powerless remnants. Lamar never entertained the thought of assimilating them into Texas society.

In 1840, twelve Comanche chiefs were invited to the Council House, or Bexar County courthouse, in San Antonio, ostensibly to discuss the ransom and return of their many captives, including first and foremost Cynthia Ann Parker. Granny Parker had never ceased calling for her Christian grandchild's return from the "heathens."

The Council House was a trap. The ransom was never intended to be paid. The Comanche broke out of the building and tried to flee to the river. Although they had come under a flag of truce that was to extend for twelve days, all twelve chiefs were killed. Among the party were women and children, some of whom died with their men. The Bexar County sheriff and an officer were killed, as was a visiting judge who was merely a witness to the battle.

An Indian woman, the widow of one of the murdered chiefs, was set free to return to the Comanche to demand the release of the Honey-Eaters' captives. She was instructed to carry the demand for surrender. Instead, when she reached the Honey-Eaters, she shrieked and howled and cut off several of her fingers in mourning. Thirteen captives who had been slated for return were roasted alive or tortured until they died.

The vow was made that day: From where the sun now stood, the Comanche nation would keep no peace with Texas.

Reprisal was swift in coming.

Three hundred Comanche led by Chief Hears the Wolf rode to San Antonio. Hears the Wolf galloped his horse into the main plaza, where he screamed insults and issued challenges, but no one faced him. The citizens huddled behind locked doors. Next he rode down the river to San José Mission, where the soldiers were, but their captain refused to fight. In contrast to the treachery of the Council House, he insisted that his men honor what remained of the truce. The captain was later called a coward and perished in the pistol duel that resulted from the insult.

With no one to fight, Hears the Wolf, along with many of the Comanche tribes as well as the Kiowa, withdrew to the High Plains, where a great council was held. At last, in August, Buffalo Hump, a surviving war chief, led a band of between four hundred and one thousand warriors on a raid that would be a show of determination and force. They moved by night under the light of a Comanche moon. Bypassing San Antonio, they galloped east and south to the old town of Victoria only twenty-five miles from the Gulf of Mexico. There, Buffalo Hump did what no Comanche had ever dared or perhaps cared to do: He took the town. While settlers sheltered in some homes in one part of town, the Comanche killed defenders who tried to oppose them, rampaged through the streets, and stole two thousand head of horses and mules.

Driving the herd before them, they rampaged on toward the gulf with the state militia companies trailing them, afraid to attack but left with the unpleasant duty of burying the mutilated bodies of the dead. On August 8 the Comanche sacked and burned the town of Linnville on Lavaca Bay. Finally, considering that he had delivered his message and obtained revenge, Buffalo Hump strapped the loot onto the backs of dozens of mules. With heavily laden animals, many prisoners, and three thousand horses, he headed back to the Llano Estacado.

He might have made it had he not been so greedy. Instead, his burdens forced him to move slowly. He was trailed by legendary frontier captains Ben McCulloch, Edward Burleson, Matthew Caldwell, and Big Foot Wallace, all of whom later became Texas Rangers. The captains and their men stampeded the great horse herd. The Comanche dispersed to try to control the animals rather than deploy for war. Horses and heavily laden mules piled up in a boggy stretch along the Colorado. Caldwell took his men around on the flank and killed every Comanche in his path. Hand-to-hand combat from horseback—lance against bowie knife, arrow against rifle—went on for fifteen miles. More than eighty Comanche were slain. In the end they lost heart and abandoned their loot to flee in disorder.

In a final insult that punished the Comanche psychologically, the Tonkawa scouts who had run for thirty miles to join the fray on the Texans' side were given citations for bravery and their pick of fine Comanche mounts. On August 13 by the light of a waning moon, the "Tonks," whom some believed were a northern branch of the despised cannibalistic Karankawas, held a victory dance. During the celebration they roasted and ate several Comanche arms and legs.

No Comanche ever rode down to the coast to attack a town again. Unfortunately, however, they resumed their guerrilla warfare, ultimately sealing their own fate. Over the next ten years, the problem of what hundreds of Texans could do against millions of Comanche remained unsolved. In 1845 Texas was annexed to the United States. The solution of the U.S. Army was to build a string of forts along the Comanche frontier. Their ineffectiveness was obvious. Troops stationed a hundred miles apart at Forts Worth, Belknap, Clark, Duncan, Davis, Stockton, and Bliss could not protect anyone except themselves.

By the light of the moon, the Comanche rode just beyond the lookouts' range, then returned without ever being seen, except by the farmer or rancher whose crops were destroyed or whose horses were rustled. Nothing had yet happened to weaken the Indian's control of the Great Plains.

Headquarters building, Fort Concho. Author photo.

At last, the U.S. Army made a treaty with the Wasps, granting them the right of sovereignty over their lands in exchange for the return of captives and the promise to steal no more horses and to trade only with licensed traders. The paper was worthless, as the Comanche soon found out, because Texas had retained control of her public lands. The U.S. government had no right to grant sovereignty to anyone in its newly annexed state.

As a result, the sniping continued as bitterly as before. But a sea change occurred, one that none of the parties involved in the treaties could ever have envisioned.

In 1849 gold was discovered in California, the far western state acquired by the United States as tribute after the Mexican War of 1845. The far-reaching social effects of this discovery changed the history of America and the history of the Comanche forever.

Out onto the Indian's prairies where farmers and ranchers with families feared to go, gold seekers streamed. Suddenly, the plains were alive with wagon trains, stagecoach lines, and the supply stations they required. Traders, eager to trade with gold seekers who had run out of provisions, established posts all along the routes. Ultimately came the railroad builders with their "hell-on-wheels" towns that moved across the country at the end of the track. The great buffalo herds were hunted by men with rifles filling larders for hundreds more men on their westward treks.

When the news of discovery of gold in California reached Europeans, they too left their homes, sailed across the Atlantic, and began the journey across the vast continent. With them they brought their diseases. While the Comanche had faced plagues before, their numbers had merely been weakened. Now the Americans crossing the plains had also reduced the numbers of buffalo, the Comanche's source of food, clothing, and shelter.

Already weakened and disheartened by what the wise among them had perceived as a fight they could not win, the terrible plagues were the last straw. The medicine man, whose healing powers increased when "he climbed a pole in his tepee and growled like a bear," was no help against smallpox, Asian cholera, and influenza. Neither could the sweat lodge or the laxatives made from willow tree bark rid the body of impurities. Paste made from boiling "certain herbs" and painting dog tracks on the patient and then on a large dog made no difference. Prayers, incantations, and ultimately the hideous mutilations and tortures of the Sun Dance proved there was no hope.

History repeated itself in the destruction of the Comanche as well as more than half of all the Indians of the Great Plains. The diseases for which most had no natural immunities killed them in record numbers. Those who were resistant starved to death as the buffalo disappeared from the plains. They were reduced to eating their dogs. Finally, they ate their horses.

By 1851 the Comanche population in Texas had dropped from twenty thousand to twelve thousand. As with the Aztecs, the leaders died, the warriors became psychologically debilitated, and the factions could not agree to act and speak with one voice.

The last fifty years of the nineteenth century marked a period of westward expansion from sea to shining sea for America the Beautiful. Oblivious to the sufferings of people whom they considered less than human beings, the settlers, the tradesmen, the miners, the town builders, and all of the numberless host trekked westward through the bones of the buffalo and the Indians who had built a culture around them.

In December 1860 Peta Nocona, chief of the Antelopes, who had so far survived because they had not come down from the Great Plains, was forced into central Texas by a terrible blizzard. He brought with him his blonde wife, Cynthia Ann Parker, Elder John Parker's granddaughter. She was the mother of his three children: Quanah, who would have been about ten at the time; Pecos, who was younger; and their baby sister, Topsannah.

Ranger Captain Sullivan Ross attacked. The Comanches scattered. The boys escaped. Their father, Peta Nocona, was never heard of again. Ross believed he was killed trying to protect Cynthia Ann. When she was attacked, her blanket was pulled off and her blonde hair streamed out in the wind. Sullivan Ross had found the most famous of all the Comanche captives. That single accomplishment more than any other led to his election as governor of Texas.

Had he foreseen her tragedy, would he have let her go? Within two years after being returned to "her family," Topsannah had died of "white man's disease," and Cynthia Ann had starved herself to death.

In 1867 the intensive slaughter of the buffalo began. The demand for buffalo robes and buffalo tongues left the prairies empty of all save rotting carcasses. American tanneries had developed a process that made the hides especially valuable. In the end American manufacturing, rather than the U.S. government, destroyed the buffalo.

By 1874, Quanah Parker, thirty-four years old, had become war chief, medicine chief, and council chief of the Antelopes and essentially of the Comanche nation. Perhaps by virtue of his genetic makeup, inherited from his mother, none of the plagues had touched him. On September 28 his last surviving band was camped in the Palo Duro Canyon in the heart of the Texas panhandle. Safe from the icy blasts of an early winter, they had allowed their horses to roam freely in the canyon that was 120 miles long and 1,000 feet deep.

Quanah Parker, last chief of the Comanche. Author collection.

The winter refuge became a trap when the Fourth Cavalry, commanded by Ranald Mackenzie, attacked. Unable to mount their animals, without extra clothing, and without food and supplies, the Comanche fled down the canyon.

Mackenzie did not even try to pursue. Why should he risk his men when the winter would take care of the Indian problem once and for all? Utterly ruthless, he gave orders to burn all the tepees and supplies. Huge stocks of flour, sugar, blankets, meat, and repeating rifles and ammunition were burned.

Then, in an act that signaled the end of the Comanche as a people as nothing else could, he separated the branded cavalry horses from the 1,424 horses rounded up out of the canyon. He allowed the Tonkawa scouts to

January in the Palo Duro Canyon; ice in the streams. Author photo.

take what animals they wanted. Then, in a thunderous roar of army rifles, 1,048 shrieking, plunging animals were destroyed.

Indomitable, Quanah led his shivering, starving people up to the Canadian River to wait for the buffalo one more time. They did not come.

In June 1875 he led all the Comanche remnants, barely a thousand souls, out of Texas to Fort Sill, Oklahoma. There he surrendered to join the ones already there. The number of Comanche remaining was 1,597. Hundreds of thousands had been killed, had starved, or had died of diseases for which they had no immunities and no peace and time to develop them.

Mirabeau Lamar's policy had succeeded. It was a true disaster—the destruction of a people. Nothing in Texas history can ever exceed it.

"Comanche Moon"
(Accompanied by Indian flute and hand drum)

'Cross the wide and windswept Llano,
Marked with bones of buffalo,
A ghostly band comes galloping,
A hundred men or so.

Pinto ponies, duns, and buckskins,
Three or four each warrior's string.
Ho! Comanche! We have claimed them,
Rustled bounty from Old Spain.

Civil chief and war chief lead them.
As their council bids them go,
By the full moon's dark moon shadow,
Ride two hundred miles or so.

Where the Wild Goose Moon above them
Casts its shadow darkly blue,
They raid for white men's horses
And for white men's rifles too.

Mark their lances couched beside them,
Strung across their backs, stout bows.
Fierce hearts leap to meet their destiny
In battle with their foes.

Though their time be gone forever,
In the sun they ride no more;
But at night when time is endless,
Hear them galloping as before.

From the Cap Rock see their dust rise;
Find their path across the snow.
By the full moon's dark moon shadow,
Ride two hundred miles or so.

3

LIKE A HOUSE OF CARDS

At six o'clock on a Saturday evening, the Angelus rang out from the tower of St. Mary's in Galveston. The cathedral was only five blocks south from the Strand, the famous street of business that bordered the bay on the leeward side of Galveston Island. St. Mary's stood seventeen blocks, a mile and a half, from the Gulf of Mexico.

Suddenly the cathedral towers swayed violently. The two-ton bell that had just tolled was torn from its iron bands and clasps and fell to the stones below.

At the same time that the bell crashed to the floor, the huge Celtic cross atop St. Patrick's Church on Broadway was ripped away. People nearby did not hear it fall. The roar of the wind and the crashing of houses, the constant clatter of slate as roofs tore off, drowned out such a minor sound as a cross plummeting two hundred feet to the shell-paved street.

The ferocious wind and the storm surge were overwhelming the island. If stone edifices so far inland were breaking up, there could be no hope for families in light, wooden beach houses closer to the waters, no hope for the orphans and nuns in St. Mary's Orphanage, no hope for the soldiers at Fort Crockett.

Clarence Howth's house was only four blocks from the beach. He had made no effort to leave. Along with almost everybody in the city, he believed that the storm would reach its height and then retreat before any real damage was done. Storms had done so before, even the devastating storm of 1875 that had brought in an 8.5-foot flood. Confident that he could ride out the hurricane, he carried his wife up into the attic along with their newborn baby. Her father, Confederate veteran Dr. John B. Sawyer,

41

*Ruins of St. Patrick's Catholic Church. Courtesy
of the Rosenberg Library, Galveston, Texas.*

her brother Ossapha, a maid, and a nurse picked up the mattress and followed.

When Clarence opened everything up downstairs, Mrs. Howth protested that her lace curtains would be soaked and ruined. He answered that a few things might get wet, but they could be replaced if they were torn. Opening everything to allow the water to flow through was the standard procedure. The structural integrity would not be appreciably damaged. At 6:00 P.M., in almost total darkness but still sure that everything would be fine, he went upstairs to the attic to join his family.

As he passed an upstairs window, Howth ventured a look out. He believed at that time that the waters were receding slightly. Earlier, they had submerged the eight-foot fence in the front yard and had blown slate off the roof. The house was leaking everywhere, but by flashes of lightning he thought he could see the top of the fence again.

He comforted his wife and reassured everyone with that piece of news. The storm would soon be over. Generally, the water would rise steadily, then recede quickly. It had left a mess, but the servants could clean it up; furniture and household goods could be replaced.

What Howth thought he recognized as the storm's end was only a brief respite. The mighty power of the wind was creating a seldom-noted phenomenon. As the hurricane closed in, the high tide never had a chance to get out. Within ten minutes it rolled back in higher than before. Dragging the sea with it, the gale struck and pushed against everything in its path.

It ripped the shutters off the house. The slate roof sheared away in a great chatter-clatter of deafening noise. Every shingle became a missile flying away in the wind to do incalculable damage farther up the island. Fleeing for their lives in water up to their shoulders, people were decapitated by the shingles. Ironically, they had been mandated by the city to prevent a recurrence of a disastrous fire in 1885 when a high wind spread incendiary ashes across the city.

Already driven into the attic by the rising water, the Howths had no higher place to climb to. Moreover, they had no roof above their heads. High water was breaking against the windows, threatening to smash the glass. Dr. Sawyer, Howth's father-in-law, pulled the mattress off the floor and tried to brace it against the window.

"Stay with the house," he shouted over his shoulder. "If she stands this five minutes, it will all be over."

The wind shifted again.

The words were hardly out of his mouth before the house fell, its walls collapsing, its floors buckling. Everything and everyone was thrown into the rushing, foaming sea.

Howth was thrown under, then tossed up. He caught hold of a window frame and floated on it. Even as he shouted in the darkness for his wife, he realized he was floating against the wind. Unable even to pray, he held on as he was carried out to sea. Helpless, in total darkness, with the wind howling past his ears, he wrapped his arms around the wreckage.

All over the city the same stories were being lived as entire families were simply swept away.

On September 8, 1900, the worst natural disaster in the history of the United States occurred. The hurricane and the resultant storm surge killed an estimated six thousand people. Subsequent research has proved that storm surges result in nine out of ten fatalities.

At the time of this devastating hurricane, the first one of its magnitude to strike a densely populated area, the U.S. Weather Bureau had made no studies of such things and consequently had no warnings or advice to issue. Ships at sea had no capabilities to send messages to the mainland of hurricanes building offshore in Cuba and heading into the Gulf of Mexico. No real measurements of storm severity existed.

Storm-surge flooding happens when hurricane winds push the water from the Gulf before them. In the case of Galveston, winds of more than one hundred miles per hour were recorded before the storm blew away the anemometer. Weathermen estimated later winds were more than 120 miles an hour, by modern measurements an F2 on the Fujita Scale, a strong storm capable of considerable damage.

Friction between the moving air and the slower water creates drag. If the hurricane is streaking across the Gulf, the farther it moves, the more water it gathers up beneath it. The water literally flattens and builds to heights greater than twenty feet. The elements race into the pocket of least resistance, a barometric low.

A 28.30 barometer reading, a low for Galveston, was noted by First Mate W. Ledden in the log of the steamer *Comino*. It drew the storm to the bay like a magnet. Normal waves did not come in and turn back out to sea. Instead, the huge monstrous rush of water rolled over the entire island, pushing everything before it.

When the water finally retreated, it pulled a great deal of what had

Storm-surge flooding on Broadway, the highest spot on the island.
Courtesy of the Rosenberg Library, Galveston, Texas.

been torn loose back to sea; then normal tidal flow brought it in again. The same phenomenon occurred with Hurricane Camille on the Gulf Coast of Mississippi and Louisiana in 1969.

In the face of such superior natural strength, man has no choice but to run for his life. He cannot stand against it.

Galveston was an island. In its long history, it had been visited by the Indians, the French, the Spanish, the rebel Texans, and the pirate Jean Lafitte. At the beginning of the twentieth century, a two-mile-long wagon bridge and three railroad bridges connected it to Virginia Point on the mainland of Texas.

On the farthest eastern tip of the island at the head of the south jetty stood Fort Point Lighthouse. On the western side at the head of the north jetty was the Bolivar Peninsula and Bolivar Lighthouse. The mouth of Galveston Bay was two miles wide, a natural ship channel named Bolivar Roads.

Since Galveston was easily one of the busiest ports on the Gulf of Mexico, the federal government had recently deepened the channel to ocean-

Ashton Villa, one of the stately homes on Broadway
miraculously left standing. Author photo.

going traffic and floated in massive granite blocks. No force on earth could have moved them.

Unfortunately, nothing had been done to protect the city at the mouth of the channel. In many ways she was a city that lived still in the nineteenth century. For example, for a city with such rich trade, Galveston's thoroughfares were a problem. The main streets were paved with wood blocks gleaned years earlier from ships' ballast. In the residential areas, streets were covered with shells that glared white in the sunlight. In poorer areas they were merely hard-packed sand.

However, no one complained. The streets of business, the main one being the Strand, were on the north side of the island facing the bay. The rest of the town, an area one and a half by five miles, was home to families both well-to-do and relatively poor. Together they enjoyed the clement weather and all the pleasures that the largest and prettiest gulf in the Western Hemisphere had to offer.

On this particular day it offered little to recommend it. By 8:00 A.M. the tide was still rising; such gutters as there were in the streets filled with water. The wind whipped the sand up from the beach hard enough to sting and cut exposed skin. A torrent of water poured through Bolivar Roads into Galveston Bay.

Seventeen ships were at anchor east and north of Galveston Island. Squalls began to strike as the morning progressed. The captain of the English steamer *Taunton* called for steam. He wanted to ease the strain on his anchor chain and have her in position to respond quickly to his command.

People with phones began to call the Weather Bureau office number, 214. The only advice to be given was get to higher ground. Although there really was no higher ground, almost no one considered leaving the island.

Indeed, people were coming onto it. At 9:45 A.M. the last train into Galveston left Houston Station fifty miles away. The passengers on the *Galveston, Houston, and Henderson* noted that the water in the bay was splashing against the rails.

By ten o'clock St. Mary's Orphanage, which sheltered ninety-three orphans with ten nuns to care for them, was completely surrounded by three feet of water. The home was located west of the city, practically on the beach. The nuns made plans to rope the orphans together in case they had to wade to higher ground.

An hour later the waves were breaking one block from Broadway, the ridge of the island, eight feet above the tide line. Still, most people had no fear. A general air of, Oh, we've seen all this before, with a stifled yawn was pervasive. The police chief, Ed Ketchum, a Yankee whom residents accepted somewhat grudgingly, sat at his desk answering the telephone and dispatching an occasional patrol wagon.

At one o'clock the train arrived from Houston. The bay over which they had passed was "a raging torrent," wrote a nurse at John Sealy Hospital, also on the Strand. When the passengers stepped down, the wind was gusting, the rain fell in sheets, and no one was there to greet them. From the terminal on the Strand, they had to wade to their destinations.

Out on the Gulf, the Pagoda Bathhouse was washed away. At about the same time, the wind began to blow the glass out of the windows. Pedestrians tried to stay under the awnings but still had to keep a "weather eye" and dodge the tiles from the slate roofs—a difficult business considering the high water. Observers recorded the wharves were submerged by the bay waters, and the ships were riding above street level.

At Fort Crockett, on the southern outskirts of the city, six miles from the north end of the Strand, the soldiers were getting worried. At two

The Strand, the downtown area on the leeward side of the island.
Courtesy of the Rosenberg Library, Galveston, Texas.

o'clock the captain sent a message to evacuate the barracks. Thirty men struck out for higher ground. Three were drowned on the way. Ten men elected to remain in the shelter of the fort.

The Cline brothers were in charge of the Weather Bureau. Isaac Cline had started out in a horse and buggy early that morning to warn people to get to higher ground. His brother Joseph wrote a telegram stating that the city was fast going under water and that great loss of life must result. He stressed the need for relief.

Joseph then carried it to the Western Union Telegraph office, three blocks south. The Strand was nearly impassable. By that time the entire pavement of wooden blocks was floating. With every step Joseph took, a block turned under his foot, and he floundered knee deep in salt water.

When he arrived, he was told that their wires were also down. As a last chance, he picked up the telephone and asked the long-distance operator to connect him with the Western Union Office in Houston. He was told that the wait would be two hours because so many were ahead of him.

In desperation, he asked for Tom Powell, the manager, who gave him a connection to Houston. Joseph filed the message, requesting that the telegraph office treat it as confidential because Houston and Galveston were rivals; he didn't want the news to get out that the city was in trouble.

At 3:00 P.M., almost the instant that Joseph's message ended, the long-distance wire snapped. Galveston was cut off. What happened from then on depended on the fury of the weather and the mercy of God.

Elsewhere on the island, the Pettibone family left their small cottage to wade to the home of a neighbor who had an upstairs. They were invited upstairs because all "sorts" of people had taken shelter in the lower rooms. Just as they reached the top of the stairs, the house settled. The ceiling fell in. By a miracle, the rafters caught on the windowsills and prevented their being crushed. They were trapped for hours in a triangular slot in wretched darkness while all around them they heard the noises of the rain and wind, the screams, and the futile cries for help.

By four o'clock Fort Crockett disintegrated into a mass of kindling. The men remaining in the barracks were all swept away along with the fort. The water was a foot deep on Broadway, the highest point on the island, fifteen feet above the shoreline at low tide. The wind reached hurricane velocity.

By five o'clock it was as dangerous to try to move to higher ground as to stay in a second-story room or in an attic. People were being struck down by flying slate. They were being knocked off their feet and slammed under the water by debris, never to be seen again. The wreckage was whirling faster than a man could run down the streets. It trailed every imaginable object from children's toys to chicken coops to parlor tables and roofs. Floating garages and sheds collected smaller pieces that turned them into lethal derelicts.

One family managed to climb up onto a roof where they floated throughout the night. Only the wife and mother was lost. When the waters had receded and they could climb down, they discovered to their horror that her drowned body had been caught and borne along beneath their makeshift raft.

In the storm the animals—horses, mules, cows, chickens, dogs, and cats—were deserted. As the police chief's son made his way through chest-deep water, he saw a floating doghouse lodged against fence. A Scottish terrier was chained to it. Although the dog barked frantically, the boy pressed on, intent on saving himself. For the rest of his life, Henry Ketchum carried a burden of guilt that he had not waded the few feet to release the animal.

People trying to get to higher ground in buggies, carts, and wagons fared no better than those on foot. The panicky animals were difficult to control. Someone had to take their heads and lead them. One man reported that when he drove his horse out of the lee of a building, the animal was blown over in the traces. Although he got the animal to its feet, it was so terrified it balked. He had to abandon it and his cart.

A bit farther on, the man reported that when his brother rounded a corner, he was blown off his feet. The water was so swift and deep that his brother couldn't get up again. People trying to walk found they could do so only by dragging themselves hand-over-hand along fences.

At 6:00 P.M. the commercial buildings began to go as the storm reached its peak. The smokestack collapsed on top of the powerhouse, killing many of the people who had taken refuge inside. The First Baptist Church's tin roof, an acceptable substitute for slate, blew off like a giant kite and slammed down in the street.

Inside the standing houses in what was left of the town, the night was a cacophony of terror. In the attics and second stories, survivors could not keep from glancing out the windows. Flashes of lightning revealed scenes that they never expected to see this side of the River Styx.

They saw people wading, swimming, struggling, and hanging on for dear life to whatever they had managed to find. The water was loaded with debris intermixed with the white forms of human bodies floating face down and animals floating belly up.

Even if they huddled in the dark as far from the windows as they could get, the night was full of hideous sounds. Above the wail and roar of the wind came the cries of terrified people seeking help, seeking loved ones, losing their reason, and screaming endlessly in panic.

The next day one little girl told the reporter from the *Galveston News* that she and her Mamma and her eight little brothers and sisters prayed incessantly for those outside and for themselves. She further said that she prayed that her Mamma above all would be saved because she and her oldest brother were too young to be mothers.

Those inside the houses kept steeling themselves as they heard and felt the almost constant thudding as timbers, pieces of houses, telephone poles, buggies, small houses, sheds, and who knew what else were driven into the lower parts of their houses.

Closer to the weather station on the southwest end of the island, the houses were badly damaged by the railroad trestle. The rails held the bridge together so that it became a two-hundred-foot-long instrument of destruction ripping into the sides of buildings and slashing at struggling survivors. On its spinning, floating path, it hooked and upset a raft with twenty-five people on it.

The entire building that housed the Lucas Terrace apartments fewer than three blocks from the beach was knocked down except for the second-floor apartment of Miss Daisy Thorne. She and her neighbors had retreated to her bedroom in the farthest southwest corner of the building. Finally, the third floor blew off and the second floor settled. But it did not wash away. At dawn Daisy and her castaways discovered what had saved them. The room directly beneath them had jammed full of floating wreckage. It literally could not collapse.

The stone churches offered little chance of salvation either to the religious communities they sheltered or to those who sought help within them. On Broadway, St. Patrick's Church, from which the Celtic cross had been ripped, was a total wreck. Water had risen in the sanctuary and torn down the walls. Indeed, a waterspout, or tornado, was probably embedded in the hurricane. Such a phenomenon might account for the terrific central damage while the towers on both ends of the building stood well enough.

In St. Mary's Cathedral four blocks south of the Strand, the Right Reverend Nicholas Gallagher, bishop of the diocese of Galveston, ordered that the priests be prepared for death. Between 7:00 and 8:00 the nuns in St. Mary's Orphanage divided their ninety-three charges and roped them to their waists. They tried to pray in the chapel on the first floor of the girls' wing, where they all saw the boy's wing collapse. Within minutes, the roof fell in on the orphanage. Only three teenage boys managed to escape. Later the body of one nun was found with her charges still roped to her waist.

On the other hand, in the massive Ursuline Convent only ten blocks from the beach, nearly one thousand people had gathered. Although the ten-foot wall around the structure crumbled, its own stone walls stood. Four expectant mothers gave birth to children that night. All the babies were christened immediately because no one expected them or their mothers to survive.

Mrs. Carrie Hughes and her daughter, as well as Mrs. Eliza Williams and her daughter, were swept out into the Gulf. The wall of a broken house had slammed into their house. As they went down, the ceiling from the wreckage hit Mrs. Hughes in the back of the head. With her daughter clinging round her neck, Mrs. Hughes climbed onto the ceiling and then dragged her friends up with her.

As they floated for what seemed like hours, Mrs. Hughes remembered the intense cold, so cold that she thought she would freeze. They lay huddled together, suffering from hypothermia and dying of thirst. The rain felt

*Temporary morgue in a cotton warehouse. Courtesy of
the Rosenberg Library, Galveston, Texas.*

like hailstones as they were whirled round and round. When her daughter tried to sit up to get a firmer grip on the raft, the wind stripped her clothing off. Possibly they too had been caught in a waterspout.

The many merchant ships anchored in the bay and tied up to the wharves fared as badly as the buildings on land. The power of the wind tore many anchors up from the bottom and carried the ships up the flooded beaches, leaving them stranded, helpless. One was literally blown up the channel broadside. Several were thrown into each other before they were grounded.

The *Comino,* whose first mate had logged the record low barometric reading, and another vessel that had remained tied up to the wharves were badly damaged by flying debris, especially the slate shingles.

The *Taunton*'s captain, who had started his engines when the blow began, felt her anchors pull up from the bottom. She was driven straight toward the Quarantine Station, but the captain's foresight saved his ship. He managed to get steerage and avoided the collision.

Finally, at 7:30 P.M. the barometer began to rise. The center of the hurricane was passing Galveston several miles to the southwest. At 8:00 P.M. the water was 15.6 feet deep at St. Mary's Infirmary. Downtown, it was 10.5 feet deep. The wind tore the iron roof off the Union Passenger Station building. The worst was over, but no one would have believed it.

In another hour the storm center was well past Galveston. The wind began to diminish, and the water began to drain out of the town as if "a tubful had been turned over." Although the wind continued to blow, it had lost its punch. Gradually, the rain ceased pounding; the wind began to die. To everyone's astonishment as they ventured outside, "a bright moon was beginning to show through the clouds."

The hurricane continued on its way, causing damage but nowhere near the amount sustained by Galveston. It traveled into Oklahoma and Kansas, turned to the northeast, and picked up power in the Great Lakes. With fresh strength it did damage in Canada before disappearing into the North Atlantic north of Halifax on Wednesday, September 12.

Clarence Howth floated back onto the sand. He had traveled out into the Gulf and back again. Naked, shivering, and exhausted, he began to weep. He had lost everything in the world except his life.

Rescue efforts began almost immediately. People who had survived in buildings downtown began to organize themselves and move out, hallooing as they went. While many were still in their badly damaged homes, one of the horrors of the rescue efforts, even as the water went down, was to discover that people were alive in and under heavy piles of wreckage. Tragically, very few were rescued before they died because the water had created such an intricate and tightly packed jam.

Freakishly, some houses remained standing and relatively undamaged close to the beach in blocks where all around them had been swept bare. Whole families and their neighbors who had sheltered with them stepped out onto their porches and looked around in horror.

The National Guard, as well as rescuers from neighboring towns, came in as soon as they could safely cross Galveston Bay, which had become a horror no one had ever seen before. Boats had to push their way through floating wreckage and hundreds of bodies.

The mayor issued an appeal "to the people of the United States." He estimated five thousand people had been killed. One third of the island's residences were destroyed. Several thousand people were homeless and destitute with no way to get off the island or even to help themselves.

Dr. William L. Crosthwait, a Texan, happened to be in Chicago at the time. He went to the newspaper for information. By luck he encountered William Randolph Hearst, millionaire publisher of the Chicago *American*. Responding to Crosthwait's pleas, Hearst started the ball rolling by placing the doctor in charge of several relief trains and writing a check for $50,000. It was an example of unparalleled largesse.

Along the southeastern beachfront of Galveston Island, twenty thousand people had lived in comfort with a sense of absolute security. Every precaution had been taken in most cases. Their houses were set eight to ten feet above the ground so that high water would roll under them. The foundations were sunk in the ground on pilings ten feet deep. They had covered their roofs in slate according to city specifications, believing the extra weight would keep their houses tight and dry. As the waters began to rise, householders opened the doors and windows in the lower floors to allow the waters to rush through and leave the upper floors and attics safe and undamaged.

None of their careful calculations and preparations did any good. The truth was that no real preparations were possible against a storm of this magnitude. Nothing stood between the residents and the water except a gentle slope. A person in good health could stroll north along Twenty-third Street, also called Tremont, hardly aware that he was going upwards. The length of his stroll would be twenty-three blocks, hardly more than two miles. The highest ground on the island was on Broadway, 8.7 feet above the Gulf.

The statistics resulting from this complacency are frightening. In a city of nearly forty thousand people, an estimated six thousand lost their lives. Where twenty thousand of those people had lived, not a house remained.

Meaningless dollar figures were bruited about to put a price on what was lost, but the highest figure could not possibly impress the reader as much as the truth of thousands of houses reduced to shattered lumber piled up against the stone foundations and walls of commercial buildings and churches where it lodged as the water receded; $28 million is an oft-quoted figure. The insurance companies paid relatively little, however, because so much of the property was either underinsured or carried no insurance at all.

Three hundred feet of shoreline, a total of fifteen hundred acres, was simply swallowed by the Gulf. Much of that land has never been recovered. The island was much reduced in size.

Albert E. Smith was one of the earliest news photographers to arrive on the scene. Smith was famous for shooting newsreel shots of the Boer War in South Africa. Since all transportation to the devastated island was forbidden except by relief agencies, he displayed a card from a New York wrecking company whose specialty was ships. He was given a permit because he said he could make arrangements to get the grounded and heavily damaged vessels afloat.

Once in Galveston he began taking pictures. His motion-picture equipment was spotted immediately by Texas guardsmen who took a dim view of photographers taking "too many pictures of nude bodies." Only by luck did he get past them. He shot his footage and was about to leave when he witnessed what he had long believed was a myth: "A man had been caught cutting fingers from bodies to get the rings," Smith recounted. "He had his pockets full. The soldiers pulled a sugar sack over his head, stood him up, and shot him."

On Wednesday, Pabst and Leinbach, wholesale grocers, displayed merchandise for sale. Many of the cans had lost their labels, but still the goods sold. The city received its first mail, but the post office could not deliver it because several mail carriers were dead, the streets were still too clogged with debris, and many of the addresses had simply disappeared. On Thursday, the *Galveston Daily News,* Texas's oldest newspaper, printed a full-sized paper. It had run off limited editions on a hand press for Sunday through Wednesday. The telegraph sent its first message at 4:16 P.M.

On Friday the banks opened. On Saturday the first streetcar made three trips in a rectangle. The mule, one of the few animals to survive the hurricane, could make no more. It was exhausted because the tracks were covered with mud and grass. On Sunday the four church buildings left relatively undamaged held services.

On Monday long-distance telephone calls started coming through. And five days later one of the railroad bridges across the bay was rebuilt. The Santa Fe arrived in Galveston at 6:20 A.M. A new day was dawning.

The schools did not open until late October. The damage, coupled with the loss of equipment and reluctance on the part of parents to let their young ones out of sight, probably created the delay. New York City school children donated almost $28,000 of the estimated $90,000 needed to rebuild and refurnish the buildings.

Three important and permanent changes occurred almost immediately as a result of the disaster.

On Sunday morning, September 9, Galveston citizens observed how the storm had formed a high barrier half a mile or more inland. Made of debris from shattered houses and outbuildings, it had been lodged against stronger structures until it formed its own structure of sorts. Particular attention was paid to Miss Daisy Thorne's remaining apartment in the Lucas Terrace. The last of the building had remained standing above a wall of wreckage. The debris, which had caused so much destruction during the storm, had formed a sort of barricade that had probably prevented everything on the island from being swept away. Two years later the city contracted to build a seawall for $1,198,318. The final amount was about half a million more than originally estimated, but no one complained. The seawall, which exists today and is the pride of Galveston, began on this site.

It was planned to stretch for six miles along the Gulf. It would be built of reinforced concrete on creosoted pilings driven forty feet into the sand. In front of the concrete would be a protective layer of granite blocks extending twenty-seven feet toward the sea. It was to be sixteen feet thick at the base and stand seventeen feet above the average low tide. It was planned to be more than a foot above the 1900 storm tide.

The second recommendation was even more staggering, but with their city in ruins around them, Galvestonians were ready for anything. The entire city was to be raised seventeen feet at the seawall to slope gradually down to the bay. A canal was to be dug. It would be the passage for hopper dredges that would suck the sand up from the bottom of the Gulf, bring it in, and discharge it through pipelines under the buildings. All this sand would raise the grade of the land and everything that remained standing on it. In all, 2,146 buildings would be jacked up for sand to be pumped underneath them. The audacity of the enterprise and the staggering expense awed the rest of the world. Why not just move away? But the people loved their city. They shrugged their shoulders, tightened their belts, and undertook the unprecedented suggestion. The largest building raised was a three-ton church. While it was boosted off the ground and fill was pumped underneath, services were not interrupted.

The third recommendation was that city government be completely overhauled. Political mismanagement had virtually bankrupted the city. It was discovered on the morning of September 8, 1900, that one of the richest cities in Texas had no money to begin repairs. Propelled by the outrageous situation, Texans swept "the bastards out" with the tide.

St. Patrick's Catholic Church restored with its Celtic cross. Author photo.

Two weeks to the day after Clarence Howth lost his young wife, his infant child, his father-in-law—a former officer of the Confederate Army—as well as his servants and all other members of his household, he wandered down toward the Gulf. Where his house had stood, where he had commiserated with his wife about her lace curtains, he found his garden hose still attached to the faucet where he had watered his garden in the backyard. Nothing else remained upon the sand.

"It seemed as a dream," Howth remembered.

But another old man remarked fifty years later, "Just don't let anybody tell you that it wasn't one hell of a storm."

"High Winds May Exist"
(Chanting accompanied by Mayan clay whistles and hand drums)

The morning's red dawn is serene and untroubled.
The horizon's obscured by gray mist.
The surf's rolling high.
No birds are in sight.
They tell me high winds may exist.

Like Hurakan's frown a mist-covered sun glows.
A brick-dust sky shimmers so clear—
His white caps awaken.
My senses are shaken.
His whisper's the wind in my ears.

Galveston's Strand stirs and stretches uncertain.
The strange sun burns off the gray mist.
The air's like a cloak;
Ancient gods hover close.
And they whisper, "High winds may exist."

From wall clouds like granite, their breath's like a scythe.
Their force drives the waves cross the sand.
The beach houses moan.
The tall palms are shorn
As the Gulf rips their roots from the land.

Stone structures and new gods all bow to the Mayan's
High winds, which none can resist,
A force we can't see,
But we feel when it breathes,
Great Hurakan's winds that exist.

4

THE DUSTY WAR

A pair of raggedy, barefoot boys squatted on the dusty prairie in front of their soddy. As a wagon and team of horses driven by an immigrant farmer slowly creaked by, they stood up.

The sun beamed down relentlessly on a boy about their age, who had elected to walk beside the wagon for a spell. Trying to make a joke out of the infernal heat, he asked, "When does it snow around here?"

The sixteen-year-old puffed out his chest. "I seen snow once."

When the stranger didn't seem impressed, the ten-year-old brother added more information. "Yeah. And it rained once, too."

Even before the cattlemen came to graze their herds over the land, the buffalo raised dust as they moved down over the High Plains of West Texas. These migrating herds damaged the prairie grasses that bore their name but did not destroy them. Their roots sank deep; they kept their grip on the land and eased the country through the cyclical climate when years went by without rain. When the buffalo were gone, the cattlemen started the destruction of the buffalo grass, with their herds that did not migrate, but grazed until the grass was gone. The ranchers saw no reason to preserve the grass. There were so many boundless acres of it.

Only when an area was "grazed over" did they move the cattle to another location. In their case, the roots remained, although the soil was more exposed and more subject to summer's unrelenting sun and winter's wild winds that blew down from the North Pole. At that time, no one observed or cared that the new grass was not so strong. It did not seem to grow back quite so fast.

Then, in the 1880s, encouraged by the railroads to settle the West, the farmers with their families moved onto the prairie by the trainload. Experimental colonies were the new way to settle. Entire communities from east of the Mississippi moved together to help and support each other in times of emergency. Some were led by snake oil salesmen eager to turn a fast dollar. Some were led by charismatic leaders eager to found their own Jerusalems.

Almost all the land in Lubbock County, for example, was settled by groups of Quakers. They had no idea that the land they were settling was any different from the land they had left in Ohio. Totally ignorant of what they faced, they watched in anguish as their plants withered in late spring when the rains didn't come.

The word "drought" had never been used at the time they bought the land from their leaders. The land was instead portrayed as "less humid," a phrase that made it sound quite attractive. The salesmen who sold barbed wire and fence posts didn't mention drought either. They were working for the railroads that charged the farmers to freight in the barbed wire, fence posts, and farm equipment. This subtle scheme was intended to finance the laying of the rails to the golden land of opportunity—California.

Enterprising men bought large blocks of land from the railroads, the public domain, and the sales of public lands. Texas had kept those lands by the terms of her annexation. A hundred years later, she was eager to get rid of them for the taxes they would bring to her treasury.

Although the cattlemen fought violent range wars against the "nesters," in the end they lost out to the fences.

The farmers flocked onto the land they first saw as a sea of grass with wildflowers growing on it. If they noted the lack of trees, they didn't know what it signified. They paid with lifesavings and borrowed more, which they were told they could easily repay with a crop or two. Too late they learned that they had been deceived.

By that time the leaders and the salesmen had moved on, and the farmers had cut the High Plains into small plots of land to be intensively farmed. As a consequence, the grass, with its deep roots, was gone forever. Turned over by the plow, all the precious moisture was exposed to the blowing dust and the relentless sunshine. The resultant soil erosion has never ceased.

Between 1886 and 1887 a hideous drought prevailed, with never-ceasing wind stirring up dust into epic storms. Not only did it stir up the dust from the barren prairies, but on an ordinary day it also brought dust from as far away as Canada. Men sweated to death trying to haul water for their

The edge of the High Plains. Fumaroles in the background,
remainders of an ancient volcanic area. Author photo.

crops. Children sickened and died in the heat. Crazed by loneliness and the alien nature of the place, women committed suicide. Some families actually starved to death. Millions of dollars were lost, and thousands of lives were blasted. There was no relief because no technology was yet available to draw water from the giant lake underneath the plains—the Ogallala Aquifer.

Not that people didn't fight back. Some planted trees in a ridiculous hope that they would attract the clouds and make rain. But the trees could not stand against the wind that bowed their trunks, tore their leaves to shreds, and broke their limbs until, finally, what remained was cut down to make fence posts or to burn instead of cow chips in the icy winters.

Very little help came from the neighbors in the colony because every family was just like every other family. They had nothing to spare. The ranchers whose land they had enclosed were contemptuous of those who could not wrest their living from the soil. They were not without pity for people in dire circumstances, but they tended to view farmers who had virtually been given their land as inept, incompetent, or simply foolish. They had no use for such people. Their attitude was that the sooner they pulled up stakes and went back where they came from, the better.

So class warfare, as well, played a memorable role in the drama of these people. The early part of the twentieth century was a tragic time. And the American psychology and spirit were profoundly scarred by the desperate conditions that turned the sea of grass to bitter dust.

A dust storm is a strong, turbulent wind with the power to carry dust aerosols for long distances. These fine particles of clay, silt, and sand are less than 1/400 inch in diameter. Although it generally moves horizontally across the land, a storm may move vertically as well. It may pick up dust in one place and deposit it in another. It may hopscotch for miles as it moves.

In areas where the winds blow at fifty or sixty miles per hour, people should take shelter before the storm hits. Otherwise, they may suffer serious damage to any exposed skin. Ultimately, they and their animals face the danger of being smothered or permanently blinded.

A dust storm may occur when the ground has little or no protective vegetation and the topography is generally flat, with no mountain ranges or canyons to break the wind. The National Weather Service warns of such a storm when the wind rises to twenty-five miles per hour and visibility is reduced to below 5/8 of a mile.

Such phenomena may cover hundreds of miles and rise hundreds of feet in the air. They are particularly prevalent sweeping down through the Great Plains in Kansas, Oklahoma, and Texas. At first they were thought to deposit the dust in places such as Dallas and Fort Worth. Now meteorologists know that these storms come from many exotic places and travel hundreds, even thousands of miles. In the twenty-first century, satellites have observed dust storms begin in China, move across the Pacific Ocean, and arrive on the California coast. Sahara dust crosses the Atlantic to reach Florida, causing high-altitude haziness.

Sometimes the storm looks like a solid wall of dust bearing down upon a landscape. When it appears, it is a truly frightening sight. It may be as high as ten thousand feet, with four thousand tons of dust per cubic mile. The winds may blow as fast as seventy-five miles an hour.

At this point the only hope for human beings is to take shelter. Driving vehicles of any kind becomes very dangerous. Pileups on highways in West Texas are common, with their accompanying injury and loss of life. Parked cars have had the paint scraped from their bodies and their windshields pitted and scarred until drivers can't see through them.

Herds of cattle on the prairies have been smothered by the dust filling their nostrils and lungs. Plants are stripped bare of leaves and blown away entirely or left to lie, flat, desiccated stems on the dry soil.

Lubbock meteorologists now include dust storms in their forecasts, warnings, and watches. Certainly, they can be as destructive as tornadoes and hurricanes. In the late winter and early spring, the High Plains and the Llano Estacado to the south are bare of vegetation or are only lightly vegetated as the seedlings sprout. At this time the conditions are conducive to soil erosion, destruction of property, and economic ruin for anyone in the agribusiness.

People from Dumas down to Big Spring watch the weather with growing apprehension. A dry norther on its way down from Canada can generate winds of up to seventy miles per hour. The very air blinds people in a few minutes. Dust masks are routinely worn by people walking out to get the morning paper. As with all Texas weather, sometimes no warning is possible. Just the down-mixing of upper-level winds can create storms in a matter of hours. Dust storms can be sucked into the upper atmosphere as the winds begin to swirl and warm, dust-laden air rises into the funnel that forms a tornado.

Much more dangerous are the thunderstorm outflows called haboobs. These can occur at any time of the year. People who live on the plains experience these in the form of walls of dust as high as ten thousand feet, mud

The incredible flatness of the plains makes them a prey to dust storms. Note the sandhill cranes eating among the sorghum grain stalks. Author photo.

rains, and black blizzards. The last are the most dramatic and the most devastating. The dust itself is so fine that instead of being knocked to the ground by the rain and snow, the aerosols settle on the droplets of water.

A Lubbock haboob in May 2001 had 95- to 105-mile-per-hour wind gusts, perilously close to an F2 tornado on the Fujita Scale. The large hail that fell out of it caused millions of dollars' worth of damage. One woman described it as "total darkness for two hours. . . . [It] blew trucks and cars off the road." In all, 256 telephone poles were blown down. Shingled roofs peeled away like sheets of paper. Tin roofs ripped off and kited down the streets, wreaking havoc as they went.

While man may suffer terribly in the face of these phenomena, they have been discovered to be an important part of nature's cycle. In 2002 scientists observed a storm as it blew across the Pacific Ocean carrying dust from China. They tested the dust and discovered it to be rich in iron. They hypothesized that it may be a vital source of nutrients for the ocean. Furthermore, iron dust from China may be a vital nutrient for Central and South American rain forests, where soil is known to be deficient due to the constant downpours that leach important elements away from their roots. When a dust storm from the Gobi Desert in Mongolia reached Hawaii, the plankton in the seas around the islands increased their productivity. The conclusion is almost inescapable. Dust storms contribute to the natural cycle of life on earth and, therefore, cannot be all bad. Just mostly.

One man has advanced a fascinating hypothesis. The more dust in the air, the colder the air becomes. Therefore, man theoretically could produce another ice age to offset the global warning he is currently producing. At present, no technology exists for this production, but as magicians say, "If you can imagine the trick, you can figure out how to do it."

No matter the stories of those who had gone before, no matter how hostile the ranchers, no matter how terrible the droughts of 1886–1887, the farmers kept coming. Part of the ideology of the American is inevitable progress. He believes that he will also better himself and in the end he will triumph against all odds.

Stubborn to a fault, some farmers remained and made a little money in the wet years. They learned to roll with the punches, to diversify. In so doing, they even had money to buy out their neighbors or take over their deserted farms for taxes. They became farmer-stockmen. In spite of hell and no water, between 1900 and 1920 the number of cultivated acres on Texas farms almost doubled.

The High Plains emerged as a region attractive to cotton farmers because it had not yet seen a boll weevil infestation, such as had come to East Texas and Deep South Texas. The Texas Agricultural Experiment Station at Lubbock developed a type of cotton that would grow well in a dry plains environment. At the same time, farmers discovered they could grow hard, red winter wheat. And everyone bought gasoline tractors to pull their disc plows.

They were producing year after year of successful crops. Despite suggestions, dire warnings, and encouraging legislation to control soil erosion, despite some government intervention, always a touchy subject with the stalwart independent breed, they continued to plant and produce successfully. Although surpluses developed and prices fell, during the 1920s all seemed very hopeful. Most believed they had triumphed.

With the new technology and Yankee stubbornness, they plowed up an area seven times the size of the state of Rhode Island.

The disaster of the 1930s on the High Plains of the panhandle can never be forgotten. The land that had just begun to be profitable essentially went dry. Indeed, the entire lean belly of the country between the Rocky Mountains and the Mississippi River was changed forever.

No record exists of another such drought in historic times, of such heat, such soil erosion, as wind swept the Texas panhandle, as well as Oklahoma and eastern New Mexico, for years. Even Joseph's biblical interpretation of Pharaoh's dream of seven lean cattle that ate the seven fat cattle pales in comparison to what happened.

In May 1934 Texas dust fell on the Mall and the White House in Washington, D.C., helping to focus federal attention on the desperate situation. As usual the solution was to establish a project and throw money at the problem.

The Dalhart Wind Erosion Control Project provided $525 million to farmers for, among other things, seed loans for new crops. They were also paid to plow lines of high ridges against the wind. Their efforts were like pouring a teacup of water onto a raging fire. By 1935 the Dust Bowl covered one hundred million acres.

Dr. Allan L. Carter, head of the English Department at Texas Technological College, wrote letters to his grandson Bruce from 1932 through 1939. On August 7, 1932, he wrote, "It has been hot as the stoke-hole of a steamer running in the tropics." He reported that the temperature had stayed at one hundred degrees all day long. In 1932 that area of the plains had fourteen dust storms.

In June 1933, the year of thirty-eight dust storms, Dr. Carter reported that rain was becoming quite a rarity. They had only two showers in Lubbock, one in the spring and one in the summer, and Arizona had not had a drop in three years.

In March 1935, the year of forty dust storms, he described how they had "nothing but fierce sandstorms, with one two Sundays ago which turned day into midnight." His wife went about with a shovel in one hand and a broom in the other and brushed out "a few buckets of dirt." He noted that one day the dust would be reddish-brown, the next yellow, the next pale gray, indicating sands coming from various parts of the Plains, rather than consistently local.

Then, in April he wrote his grandson, "this afternoon saw massive columns of dirt ascending the sky like so many alter [*sic*] fires of the giants. The novelty of these storms has long since worn off, and the grim desolation of the country is terrifying even stout hearts."

In Amarillo 125 miles north, the storms that Carter describes occurred for a total of 908 hours—more than thirty-seven days. Seven times during January, February, and March, the visibility was zero. Once, impenetrable, dusty darkness lasted for eleven hours. One storm raged for three and a half days.

April 14, 1935, the most notorious of the black blizzards occurred. Sudden, violent turbulence accompanied a polar air mass streaking into the area. It contained lightning that forked in all directions about the bowl of the sky. The wind began a cold boil, lifting the dirt higher and higher into the air. In total darkness sometimes pierced by lightning, and deafened by thunder, the farmers and ranchers endured. These times were separated by hours of eerie silence.

No one could doubt as the blizzards blew themselves out that the region's fine soils had been swept away. And the worst was yet to come. In 1936, farmers and stockmen endured sixty-eight storms that spread throughout the region; in 1937, seventy-two; and in 1938, sixty-one. Between 1935 and 1937, one third of the farmers gave up their homes and left the area.

Novelists wrote about the ordeal more tellingly than historians. John Steinbeck wrote his epic *The Grapes of Wrath* in 1939. In 1940 John Ford made the book into a movie that won him the Academy Award for Best Director. The movie's ending was a hopeful one, with an actor closely resembling President Franklin D. Roosevelt welcoming the Okies to California with a cheerful smile. This was not the same ending that Steinbeck wrote, a grim polemic against the abuse of the land and the cruelty of man to his unfortunate brethren.

In May 1938, when Steinbeck must have been finishing his tale of the Joads' tragic ordeals, Dr. Carter wrote to his grandson, "Just last night, for instance, a biting norther started in at sunset, and rolled great masses of tawny dirt over the city as the temperature slid down to almost freezing."

"Summer is here with its temperatures of one hundred degrees daily," he wrote six weeks later. Until his death in 1939, Dr. Carter continued to mention the weather as extremes of cold and hot. In that year the region had thirty dust storms.

During the 1940s conditions improved, principally because farmers of the High Plains began tapping into the Ogallala Aquifer, the largest accumulation of water-bearing layers of rock, sand, and gravel in North America. The southern-most segment, about one third of the whole, lies under all or part of forty-six counties in the panhandle. In other words, the hot, dry High Plains of Texas sit on an underground lake of generally fresh water.

From the Plains it stretches northward, an acreage of water so vast that "millions of gallons" cannot describe it. Unfortunately for Texas, New Mexico, the Oklahoma panhandle, and parts of Kansas, they sit on the shallowest part of the lake. The deepest water rests under Nebraska, whose town Ogallala gives the aquifer its name.

Shortly after World War II, with memories of the Dust Bowl haunting their nights, the panhandle farmers began tapping it extensively. With new equipment technology and readily available financing for veterans, the precious aquifer was treated as so many American resources had been treated in the nineteenth century. Deep wells were drilled, and the water pumped out was spread around as if it would never be exhausted.

Like the oil from Spindletop and East Texas, much of the water was wasted. Sprinkler systems sprayed it into the air where much of it evaporated before it touched the ground. Open canals and trenches transported it to the field, again allowing evaporation in the hot sun. Neither the oil from Spindletop nor the water from the Ogallala Aquifer can ever be replaced. The difference is that man can live without oil.

The drought years of the 1950s were a snap for the farmers despite a near repeat of the terrible dust storms of the 1930s and all their attendant horror. With the water from the aquifer, they could replace what the hot wind had carried away. Feeling no need to conserve when so much was literally under their feet, farmers began to irrigate crops that had been planted to produce in dry conditions to increase their crop yield. Grain sorghum had become an important crop in Texas because of its ability to produce on dry land. It became vastly more important when farmers discovered how much more it produced when watered from the aquifer and fertilized with ammonium nitrate fertilizers.

Encouraged by their results with irrigation and fertilizer, farmers were dissatisfied with growing grain sorghums. Other crops promised a higher payoff. That these crops demanded water and richer delta soils did not deter them. They had the aquifer, and ammonium nitrate was cheap. They began to grow commercial vegetables, sunflowers, sugar beets, and soybeans, which normally grow in the humid upper coastal plain. Corn, especially hard on soil, began to be planted again.

Despite redoubled efforts to prevent them, the dust storms came again in the winter of 1965. The worst dust storm since records were kept of such things occurred on January 25. Winds gusted up to seventy-five miles per hour at Lubbock. Dust billowed to thirty-one thousand feet in the area from New Mexico to Abilene, almost the entire width of the panhandle. People in Muleshoe, Seminole, and Plains only a few miles from the state line suffered when ground visibility was reduced to the length of a football field.

The rain gauge in Reese Air Force Base in Lubbock had three inches of fine sand. Three inches of precious topsoil was headed out of the area. As with tornadoes and hurricanes, in the face of dust storms man has little chance to protect that which is most important to him, his land.

In 1979, with a third of all Texas land in production, 87 percent of irrigated land was located on the High Plains. Farmers there received approximately 40 percent of the state's cash crops. "The farmers and the cowmen can be friends," as they sang in the musical *Oklahoma,* when entrepreneurs began to build feedlots. How much more efficient to raise and fatten cattle and hogs on the High Plains in lots literally in the middle of cornfields!

In no time at all, the feedlot capacity became such that several thousand beef cattle could be fed up. Three million head were being marketed annually, and 70 percent of the cattle being fattened in the nation came from the High Plains. Texas boasted that she was again the leader in cattle production in the nation.

And the water was pumped out of the aquifer in greater and greater amounts.

In 2002, more than fifty years since the first drill broke through into the aquifer, at the same time that rolling dust storms were arriving in Dallas and Fort Worth, conservationists and water specialists all over the state quite suddenly began to call the Ogallala endangered. Half of the original ground water has already been pumped from it. And most of this mining has taken place in the last fifty years.

The term "mined" is significant because it should mean to everyone that water is an expendable commodity like oil and gas. It means that once it is taken out, it is gone forever. If Spindletop were a cow milked too often until she went dry, the Ogallala Aquifer may also be such a cow.

The Ogallala is different from other aquifers in Texas. It lies under a caprock of resistant caliche in multiple layers. Caliche is generally made of carbonate and silica, neither of which is water soluble. It is so tightly packed together and melded that water and other liquids cannot pass through it.

The Edwards Aquifer from which San Antonio draws its water can sink to alarming levels. Then a good rain in the Frio and Nueces river watersheds will recharge it and start it rising again. The soils above it are porous, and water begins to trickle down almost as soon as it strikes the ground.

In the Ogallala, where water levels are declining at the rate of two feet a year, the annual natural recharge rate is as little as one tenth of an inch.

Besides the profligate use of water for growing populations in large cities and for agribusiness industries, some ranchers and farmers are actually thinking of selling their water. Distant urban areas are already cringing before the shadow of "four before flushing" and "taking showers together," as California cities begged of their citizens a few years ago.

Roberts County has only one very small town on its southeastern corner. The closest town of any size is Pampa, farther south in Gray County. Roberts is the home of T. Boone Pickens's Mesa Vista Ranch. For years this steward of the land has run cattle on native grasses. At the same time, he has set in place practices that have made Mesa Vista an excellent model for range and wildlife management.

Now he is negotiating to pump water from the aquifer and sell it to distant urban areas. When conservationists decry this practice, he argues that across the county lines, farmers are already selling their water rights for extra money, thereby reducing the water underneath his land. The city of Amarillo one hundred miles away has bought seventy-one thousand acres in Roberts County adjacent to his ranch. It plans to drill forty wells to ensure a supply of water for the 175,000 people who live there. Pickens feels that he is entitled to sell his water, just as they are selling theirs, rather than have it siphoned out from under him.

But for how long can those wells continue to produce?

The water belongs to everybody, but what will be done when the aquifer can no longer produce any water for anybody? How long until the dust storms blow without ceasing, and the Garden of Eden on the hot prairie turns into a hell?

Even the most ambitious conservation plans project that the water will run out by 2050. In the lifetimes of half the people living on the High Plains today, the water will be gone. Perhaps it will be gone even sooner in big towns such as Lubbock and Amarillo. Perhaps it will be gone very soon indeed for Midland, Odessa, and Big Spring, which take their water from the very edge of the aquifer.

Long before 2050 the farmers will probably have backed out of the equation. Each gallon of water is more costly than the gallon before. With agriculture prices generally flat, the time will come in the very near future when they can no longer afford to pump water. Gasoline and electricity cost money too. When those costs become prohibitive, no one will pump.

How long before the cost of utilities in those cities, too, becomes prohibitive? When bills cost more than house payments? Perhaps in the foreseeable future these towns will be applying to far away communities and water districts for a miserable share of their water. The future is incredibly bleak for all in the western and central part of Texas unless measures beyond any known at this time are instituted. Water, the very stuff of life, is being pulled from the nine major and sixteen minor aquifers under the various regions of Texas. Entire river systems, including the mighty Rio Grande and the Pecos, are being managed and diverted.

Two hundred major dams have been constructed in Texas to provide flood control and municipal water systems. Whereas in 1913 Texans had only eight reservoirs, today they have more square miles of inland water than any other state except Minnesota, the land of ten thousand lakes. If new reservoirs now in the planning stages are built, Texas will pass Minnesota within the next twenty years.

Yet, in the end, Texans cannot manufacture more water than the snows and rains allow. Unless extreme measures are taken, measures no one has even suggested yet to the burgeoning populations of cities and towns, nine hundred Texas cities will not have enough water to meet their needs in 2050, when the state's population is expected to double from twenty million to forty million. By 2050 7.5 million acre-feet of water will be unobtainable from any source.

Beneath the High Plains the Ogallala Aquifer will no longer flow. In the words of Elmer Kelton, legendary Texas author of *The Time It Never Rained,* "It is easy, though painful, to visualize a future when Texas irrigated farming will be only a memory, and towns and cities will send delegations to Austin to fight over depleted remnants of Texas groundwater."

"Dust Storm"
(Sprightly. A banjo tune)

I believe 'twas fifty-seven,
Or was it fifty-eight?
Don't seem to make no difference.
The rains kept comin' late.
They didn't come in winter;
They didn't come in spring.
By the time we planted cotton,
We couldn't raise a thing.

Heat lightnin' on the skyline,
Dust devils on the path,
'Cause when it's dry in Texas,
It's another *Grapes of Wrath*.

"If I was asked which one I'd choose,"
Phil Sheridan did tell,
"Between the Big Bend Chisos
Or Erebus in hell,
I wouldn't think it over
'Bout where I'd choose to dwell.
I'd rent out all of Texas
And make my home in hell."

Yeah! Lightnin' on the skyline,
Dust devils by the well,
Let's rent out all of Texas
And make our homes in hell.

The dust blew east and north and south,
But mostly in my face.
Three inches in the rain-gauge
At Dyess Air Force Base,
From Dumas down to Big Spring
Was all about the same.
We'd thrown the dice and gambled.
That time we lost the game.

There's lightnin' on the skyline,
But nary a drop to tell.
We better rent out Texas
And plant cotton down in hell.

The fall it did come early
When an icy norther blew.
It rustled through the inch-wide cracks
Where nothin' ever grew.
And when we saw it comin',
We knew we'd all gone bust,
'Cause what was comin', brother,
Was a sky of goldurn dust.

There's lightnin' on the skyline,
But guess I'll rest a spell.
My farm's done gone to Dallas
And left me here in hell.

Yeah! My farm's done gone to Dallas
And left me here in hell.

5

HOLOCAUST AT WACO

A t noon on Monday, May 18, 1993, millions of Americans turned on the news all across America to witness a disaster of apocalyptic proportions. Many glanced at their remotes wondering for an instant if they had somehow found an old movie, perhaps a World War II setting with American soldiers knocking down a rural outpost somewhere in Germany.

What they were witnessing in real time, live, was not a movie. It was happening one hundred miles south of Dallas, Texas, a few miles outside Waco, the home of Baylor University, owned by the Southern Baptist Church; Waco—one of the most upright, most all-American cities in Texas. There must be some mistake. American tanks couldn't be attacking a building, breaking down the walls, using their cannons to push through the roofs of buildings in a seventy-seven-acre compound about the size of an average city block.

The announcer reported that Janet Reno, the attorney general of the United States of America, had ordered the attack on a compound belonging to a religious sect with a one-hundred-year-old history. In the land of the free and the home of the brave, where the very first article in the Bill of Rights clearly states that "Congress shall make no law respecting an establishment of religion, or prohibiting the free exercise thereof," an attorney general appointed by the president with the consent of Congress was prohibiting the exercise of religion.

Tanks were attacking a religious compound!

Everyone watching across the United States must have been thinking how wrong, wrong, wrong this was. The camera took another angle to show another tank rolling over a shiny black Camaro parked on the grounds close to the entrance. Why were they destroying a man's car? What was going on here?

No one knew that the tanks had been at work assaulting the compound and tearing down surrounding buildings for six hours. CS gas had been sprayed into the two-story dormitory-like building at 6:00 A.M., when women and little children were sleeping or perhaps at prayer.

CS, or O-chlorobenzylidenemalononitrile, is supposedly nonlethal unless people have asthmas or allergies that involve the nasal passages. For those who have nasal passages of steel, it causes choking, dizziness from lack of air, and copious weeping. It's also caustic to delicate skin if not washed off rapidly.

A government agent had awakened the sleepers over the loudspeaker. "This is not an assault! Do not fire! Exit the compound and follow instructions!"

But no one had come out. Under orders to keep up the attack, the Federal Bureau of Investigation (FBI) had been doing so for six full hours.

With television cameras from all the major networks trained on them the entire time and with newscasters from all over the state broadcasting reports to an astounded nation and the world, the situation had long gone past embarrassing. The FBI had been frustrated for fifty-one days. Now they were angry. But these were religious people. The majority were women and children.

Ever conscious of the press and its power, the FBI, under the command of Attorney General Reno, must have wanted to make a good impression. Surely, nobody expected what was about to happen.

A few minutes after noon, a plume of smoke rose from one end of the long building. From the opposite end came a second wisp. The building was afire. Both wisps turned to columns and then billows of black smoke. A white banner waving from a flagpole stood out starkly against the blackness.

To the thousands watching on the television, more than half thought the FBI had set the building afire to smoke the occupants out. But no one came out. The banner was standing out straight from the flagpole. The wind must have been blowing at least twenty-five miles an hour.

Everyone knew the compound had been under siege for fifty-one days. During that time the FBI had played loud music and kept the compound bathed in light to compel surrender. Inside, the occupants must have packed bales of hay along the windows and up over the openings. Were they trapped? Could they even get out? Why didn't they come out?

Smoke poured from more openings as the fire seemed to race through the building.

Suddenly, a man appeared on the rooftop. He spread his hands as if to say, "See what you've done." He sat down on the rooftop as if he intended to remain there and burn to death. Very shortly, the heat became too intense. If he had intended martyrdom, he had thought better of it. He jumped for his life, fell, and then picked himself up. Another figure walked into the camera range. Two men.

Only two. Where were the women and the children? The children? Where were the children?

The compound exploded into flame.

As the video cameras kept rolling, the rapt national audience heard explosions and sounds like shooting. Everyone had been told the people inside had stockpiles of ammunition as well as explosive supplies of all sorts stored in some of the rooms. They must have caught fire.

The children. The children!

At the foot of the mountain of roiling black smoke, the flames roared up around the flagpole. The white flag whipped away and disappeared in the inferno. In twenty-eight minutes the conflagration began to die.

Whatever had been alive in the building was surely dead now.

Ten minutes later, the fire trucks and other emergency vehicles from Waco, Bellmead, Axtell, Hallsburg, and Mart, none more than ten minutes away, began to arrive. Obviously, they had not been called until the building was almost completely destroyed. Why? Had no FBI members called them when the smoke first appeared? Had they believed until much, much too late that the eighty or so people inside would come running out of the building? Had they simply watched as stupefied as the millions of television viewers at the holocaust before them?

How could this have happened in Waco, Texas, "Jerusalem on the Brazos," home of the largest Baptist congregation in the world? This pleasant city was home to thousands of good people with strong religious convictions and a firm belief in the right to worship as they pleased.

Who had brought these people together to perish for their beliefs? Surely this attack will be forever regarded as one of the most disastrous events in American history.

Common to all societies are institutions that man constructs independently. One of these is religion. Among the most primitive peoples, evidence exists of attempts to preserve the body for its immortality, perhaps so the eternal spirit will have a place to return to at some later point. They designate certain people to predict and to seek to control nature to bring rain, increased fertility, and success in hunting animals.

Even in an age of space exploration, many choose not to look to those heavens. Instead, they return to simple pastoral ways and choose a charismatic master to guide them and instruct them in daily living. In the most extreme forms, these people join cults where they swiftly become dependent solely on the leader.

One of the first techniques employed by cult leaders, whether consciously or unconsciously, is to separate the men from the women. Husbands from wives, brothers from sisters. If they are married, they no longer sleep together. They no longer eat together. They no longer discuss things between themselves. In this manner each one's strongest ally is gone. They must turn to the leader for their love and support.

Women are often attracted to the leader and accept him as their sexual partner if he asks. Since the sexual act can be an act of dominance, the relationship becomes symbiotic. Paradoxically, the leader becomes as trapped as the follower. The dominant cannot exist without the submissive.

If whole families join the cult, the leader will separate the children from their natural mothers to be reared by other mothers who will "be more stern and even handed." The natural mother must depend on the leader for the love and bonding that would be hers naturally with her child. Unfortunately, such children grow up without love, strongly disciplined and never indulged. They often become quietly submissive, without initiative, or dangerously angry. For the men, their lack of a partner is explained by the leader as freedom from distraction. They can now focus on the important things that God, through the leader, wants them to do.

As a leader becomes more nearly absolute in his power, he tests his control outrageously. At first, he demands ordeals of his flock, a term associated with sheep or chicken. They must stay up all night listening to him preach and then in the morning go about their daily regimen. Their brains are too exhausted to think. Of course, the leader "meditates" and "prays" during the day, so he will be inspired for the repeated lectures at night.

Lack of sleep, separation and isolation, short rations, hard labor, and indoctrination are all brainwashing techniques. Anyone who has ever read George Orwell's *1984* would recognize Big Brother in the guru-leader of Mt. Carmel.

Vernon Howell was born in Richardson, just north of Dallas, in 1960. Reports about his intelligence and character vary. He was undoubtedly good-looking, clever, and articulate. Sympathizers maintain that he memorized the New Testament when he was only twelve. Detractors report that he was dyslexic and a poor writer whose fifty-five-minute sermon read on the radio and television was deeply edited by Steve Schneider, his second in command.

Nevertheless, he was glib enough to hold his own in any religious argument, especially when he threw scripture at his interlocutors machine-gun style. If he had not settled into the role of cult leader, he would have made a great courtroom lawyer or television evangelist.

With his ability to persuade, he had already learned that he could charm people, particularly women. As leader of the group, he could take advantage of almost as many women as he desired. And as his power grew, he wanted more and more.

Most people going about the business of associating with others at work and at leisure will never understand why kind men and women can allow religion to dominate their lives so totally. How can they allow invasions of their marriages and mistreatment of their spouses, whom they claim to love and cherish?

Perhaps they feared the end of the world established in their minds by Vernon Howell's predecessors.

The Branch Davidians had a one-hundred-year-old history that had undergone many manifestations. It was a splinter group of the Seventh-Day Adventists, who observe Saturday as their Sabbath. Their first leader, a Bulgarian named Victor Houteff, carried a staff he called The Shepherd's Rod, which he presented to his flock as a symbol of the faith. Later, another leader, Benjamin Roden, discarded the rod. He claimed therefore to be a branch of that rod. The branch, he claimed, would put forth flowers and new growth. It symbolized the new strength of the faithful.

Roden declared himself a successor to the biblical King David. Hence, the new name for the sect—the Branch Davidians. The Persian Emperor Cyrus, who defeated Babylon and freed the Jews from captivity in 539 B.C., was of special interest to him.

Roden had foretold that only a certain number of the people on earth would be accepted into the Kingdom of God. The Branch Davidians were that chosen group. Likewise, God had set a number—144,000. Of all the people on earth, only 144,000 would be saved, and only through the leader could they be taken up to Heaven. The rest would be destroyed forever. A powerful incentive to remain with the cult is the belief that only a limited number will be saved, regardless of the sorts of lives they live.

When Vernon Howell joined the group, he did not immediately supplant Roden, but he adopted David Koresh as his new name. Koresh was Hebrew for Cyrus. He named his first son Cyrus. The boy's mother was one of the young converts that Koresh had taken to his bed although he never married her.

The new David Koresh planned to be a rock musician some day. Or perhaps he had tried to be a rock musician and lacked sufficient talent. Whether he felt a religious calling or was merely taking advantage of the large donations to the group to travel and seek venues for his talent will never be known.

For several years he traveled to California, to England, and to Australia, converting people to his sect and persuading them to give all their goods and money to him and return to Waco, Texas, to live in a dormitory on an old farmstead. His charismatic personality attracted many until he had almost two hundred people living with him.

The Bureau of Alcohol, Tobacco, and Firearms (ATF) has a long and distinguished history. It is also the least appreciated in some circles and the most despised of all the branches of law enforcement. Especially in Texas, where the right to bear arms is underscored by the Concealed Handgun Law and where the National Rifle Association is strong, people have no use for the ATF.

In 1791 Alexander Hamilton instituted the bureau's parent organization to collect the federal tax on whiskey. This set off the Whiskey Rebellion in Pennsylvania. Later, its officers became "revenuers" who busted the moonshine stills of the "poor ol' farmers" of Appalachia in the early 1800s. They were Eliot Ness and his crew of "mostly Untouchables" who went after Al Capone.

Not until 1942 did they take on the assignment of enforcing federal laws regulating the ownership, purchase, sale, and use of firearms. With the addition of regulating tobacco to their chores, they reached a new low in the estimation of a very vocal segment of American society made up primarily of young men. In addition to smoking and drinking, this particular element of society is most likely to purchase and use firearms.

The United States is a nation of guns. Powerful groups assume absolutely adamantine positions about them.

The bureau became more and more unpopular as raids to enforce the laws ran into conflict with people who thought the entire bureau was a violation of the First and Second Amendments to the Constitution.

Then the order came down from Attorney General Reno to raid Mt. Carmel, whose name David Koresh had changed to Ranch Apocalypse.

Reports of child abuse were circulated everywhere. The weapons and ammunition reportedly stored there were the ATF's real target. When the raid went bad, the excuses began to fly. While all the weapons known to have been purchased were legal, Shooters Equipment in South Carolina had sold cultists parts to convert semiautomatic weapons to fully automatic ones. Another illegal sale of parts to convert AR-15s to M-16 .223-caliber assault rifles had been made to an auto shop, Mag Bag, a few miles from the compound. An ATF search warrant executed there found nothing but a few shotgun shells.

As the investigation heated up, rumors grew. A methamphetamine lab was being operated by the Branch-Davidians. Big-time drug deals were going down out the back door. They were a money-laundering operation. Perhaps the wildest rumor was that they planned to attack Waco. All these events were supposed to take place because, according to David Koresh, the Second Coming would turn into the Apocalypse.

Still, no one in the ATF seems to have conducted a thorough investigation of these accusations beyond the sales of weapons-conversion kits.

A typical day for the Branch Davidians began with prayer and Bible study. During that period David Koresh almost never put in an appearance. His apartment was the only room in the building with a television, a radio, a stereo, electronic equipment, and air-conditioning. His habit was to sleep until two or three o'clock, for he stayed up most of the night playing his electronic music or preaching or reading to his exhausted flock. Sometimes he kept them listening to him for eight hours straight.

While the women set about bathing and caring for the children, performing kitchen duties, and gardening, the men went outside for calisthenics and to run an obstacle course designed by Koresh himself. They shouted rhymes and cadence counts in military style, for he had told them they were the "Mighty Men" who guarded King Solomon's bed in the Bible and God's Marines. In the main, his short rations kept them malnourished and thin.

When the men had finished, they went to eat, and the women went out to run the course. Both men and women took their turns with legal M-16 rifles on the four-story watchtower. It was the tallest building in Ranch Apocalypse, with a 360-degree view of the compound. The ATF would later claim that it was a sniper's outpost. The court at the hearing that followed the tragedy instructed that it be identified as the water-storage tank for drinking and sanitation.

David Koresh claimed for the benefit of the *Waco Tribune-Herald* that if the Bible was the truth, then he was Christ. Since he had a firm belief in the Bible, he averred that being Christ was "no big deal." He was also quoted as saying, "Neither the ATF or the National Guard will ever get me. They are coming: the time has come."

The ATF was issued warrants based on affidavits stating that agents could be met with the following weapons: a stockpiled arsenal worth nearly $200,000, legal weapons converted to automatics for rapid fire, gunpowder, ammo, hand grenades, chemicals for manufacturing explosives, starlight filters to pick out targets in the dark, and model airplanes capable of delivering explosive charges and becoming flying bombs.

Early on Sunday morning, February 28, 1993, the ATF troops made their move, dressed in military-style fatigues, camouflage greens, blue jumpsuits with deep, flapped pockets for ammo clips, flak jackets, combat boots, helmets, and caps. On the backs of their jackets and shirts were the words "ATF AGENT" in yellow and white block letters.

To serve a warrant on a religious compound to rescue little children from abuse and institute a search for illegal weapons, they had the following: Smith & Wesson .357s, Smith & Wesson .38s, 9-mm semiautomatic pistols, Remington 870 pump-action 12-gauge shotguns, Ruger mini-14 semiautomatic rifles, Winchester 70 sniper rifles, and Heckler & Koch submachine guns. To say the ATF was ready for anything was an understatement, yet their planning was strangely lacking if they truly believed the Davidians had half the arsenal listed above.

They had decided to launch their attack during the morning prayer service because the women and children would be separated from the men, who would probably not have their weapons at hand. It was to have taken thirteen seconds to take control of the arsenal, cut off and protect the women and children, and neutralize and capture Koresh and his male followers. In twenty-two seconds—about the time required to recite "The Lord's Prayer"—a team would have scaled aluminum ladders to the second-story window and entered the main armory.

Uncharacteristically, David Koresh was up that morning, spouting scripture, organizing his defense, and exhorting his Mighty Men. Without doubt, he knew the attack was imminent.

Everyone else in town certainly seemed to.

Someone had tipped off Channel KWTX-TV, which had sent

reporter John McLemore and a cameraman. A reporter and a photographer from the *Tribune-Herald* were also parked on Farm Road 2491, a quarter of a mile from the commune. They had been waiting since 7:00 A.M. Whether the reporter was the one who had begun the series of articles that had dubbed Koresh the "Sinful Messiah" is unknown.

From their point, they could watch a Texas National Guard Sikorsky Blackhawk helicopter and two Apaches take up positions over the compound. Undoubtedly, the Branch Davidians had seen them too.

Although nothing was ever admitted, possibly this attack was planned as a show of strength to the nation—a successful mission carried out with no loss of life, no injuries, compassionate care for children and women, a dangerous cult disbanded, and an impressive feather in the cap of the new attorney general as well as the new president, Bill Clinton.

Finally, at 9:55 A.M. an ATF agent walked up to the door of the compound. Before he could knock, Koresh himself opened the door. He was dressed all in black and appeared to be unarmed.

"Federal agents with a search warrant," the ATF man growled.

Koresh lurched back and slammed the double doors shut.

ATF raiders began yelling in prescribed verbal assault mode.

Then all hell broke loose. Instant resistance came in the form of a hail of gunfire so fierce that the agents were the ones completely disoriented. Only when their companions began to fall did they realize that the gunfire was coming through the walls and windows in front of them.

Who fired first will never be known. The ATF agents found themselves in the midst of a furious firefight in which their enemy was well protected while they were exposed.

The agents who burst into the second-floor window to secure the weapons cache were hit. They had evidently brought their own cameraman, who filmed them climbing in through the window. When the cultists started shooting through the walls of the other rooms, all the noise, screaming, and confusion that followed were also recorded. Later, national television showed the scenes over and over again.

Within minutes the ATF troops were running for their lives. The medics they had brought for the cultists ran forward to collect the wounded and dying. What sounded like a .50-caliber heavy machine gun opened up. A devastating weapon, it can shoot down airplanes. Some of the cultists, dressed in ski masks, hoods, and black pajama outfits like Vietcong climbed out on the rooftops and kept up the fusillade.

Three hundred yards down the road, the journalists became the targets.

New chapel erected by the Branch Davidians. Courtesy of Ruth Welch.

Memorial to slain ATF officers. Courtesy of Ruth Welch.

David Koresh's motorcycle, on which he gave his children rides up and down the road. Courtesy of Ruth Welch.

Bus burned in 1995, two years after the siege. Courtesy of Ruth Welch.

Memorial stone of David Koresh. Courtesy of Ruth Welch.

Memorial stone of Star Howell, six-year-old daughter of David Koresh.
Courtesy of Ruth Welch.

Memorial cenotaph to the Branch Davidians donated by the Northeast Texas Regional Militia. Courtesy of Ruth Welch.

Memorial trees planted for each one who died. Courtesy of Ruth Welch.

Rubble close to the shelter Koresh had built. Note child's wagon beside the lawn mower. Courtesy of Ruth Welch.

Bus burned during siege. Courtesy of Ruth Welch.

Shelter entrance, never used. Courtesy of Ruth Welch.

One of several rubble sites in the field around the compound. Courtesy of Ruth Welch.

Heavy tarpaper covers the roof of the unfinished shelter. The odor of smoke rises on a hot afternoon. Courtesy of Ruth Welch.

Monument stands in front of the new chapel. Courtesy of Ruth Welch.

Their cars were no protection. They quickly rolled out of them but kept their cameras rolling and their reactions coming into their handheld recorders. When the fleeing agents reached them, the reporters were ordered to leave, but they remained, their video rolling, risking their lives rather than miss the chance of a lifetime.

Of course, they could not know that inside the building, the scene was just as hellish. Women and children hid crying and screaming under mattresses. The halls were filled with blue smoke. Bullets chewed huge chunks out of the walls and furnishings.

Inside, David Koresh was wounded in the side in the first blast, then later in the hand when he lurched into another room. Judy, the wife of Koresh's top lieutenant, Steven Schneider, and part of Koresh's harem, was wounded in the shoulder and right hand.

ATF snipers began to pick off the black costumed cultists on the roof to cover the ignominious rout. As one group of wounded staggered by the TV and newspapermen's vehicles, an agent yelled, "Hey, TV man, call for an ambulance!"

McLemore sprinted across an open space toward his truck. He slid down inside and began radioing for help as bullets pinged off the vehicle's side.

The fight went on for another three quarters of an hour, until a senior agent managed to get through to the compound by telephone and arrange a cease-fire. At noon a truce was called for the ATF to evacuate their dead and injured.

In the end, four ATF agents were killed, and an uncertain number were wounded, some seriously. It was a terrible day for law enforcement, and it had been recorded on television before the world.

In Waco, Texas, once known as Six-Shooter Junction, less than generous folk shrugged their shoulders. As a pickup-truck driver was heard to remark, "We're talking about Waco! If someone comes in your house blazing away, cops or whoever they are, you're gonna do some shootin' back."

Within hours the standoff began. Negotiations between David Koresh and the government of the United States would go on until both sides were frustrated beyond belief and the American people had vacillated from one side to the other and back again.

Conversations between the negotiators and Koresh at first consisted of his expressions of pain because of the wounds he had received. Still he demanded that station KRLD in Dallas–Fort Worth broadcast a statement from him. He named KRLD because it was one of his favorite stations.

The ATF asked that it broadcast their demand that the cultists should give up peacefully. Koresh demanded that he be allowed to broadcast portions of the scriptures. He promised he would allow two children to leave the compound each time one of his harangues was aired. At 7:00 P.M. the broadcasts began.

While the scripture readings were going on, Koresh contacted CNN to broadcast a live interview punctuated by his frequent groans and moans of pain. He said that a two-year-old girl, his own daughter, had been killed. Later, he said he had been mistaken. He told about calling his mother in Chandler, Texas. He blamed the ATF for everything. Although he had weapons, he denied that he ever meant to use them.

Meanwhile, KRLD was upset that Koresh had given CNN the interview, while they were broadcasting his interminable scripture broadcasts, undoubtedly from tapes made of his various sermons and prayer meetings held within the compound. They prevailed upon Koresh to give them an exclusive interview.

With a baby crying in the background, he managed to force out the words, "I've been shot. I'm bleeding bad. I'm going home. I'm going back to my father."

Two children were allowed to leave and taken immediately into social services. Shortly thereafter, two more were released. Negotiators were cautiously hopeful.

Meanwhile, ATF agents from cities around the South and Southwest began arriving, as did dozens of Texas Rangers, a bomb squad, an elite weapons team, an FBI hostage rescue team from Quantico, and an armored personnel carrier. More than three hundred law officers in all were gathered there.

The chess game between the lawmen and the "Sinful Messiah" began, with only one possible ending. Did David Koresh imagine that he saw a way out of the dilemma? Did he really expect that if he held on long enough, the government would go away, forgetting four dead agents?

Or had he come to believe his own line? Had he decided to exact the ultimate test of his control over his people by demanding what he had warned the children about? Had he decided that they would all "go home to the father together"?

Almost immediately, the criticism began from the townspeople. In Texas, where the love of football is almost as strong as the love of guns, there was endless "Monday morning quarterbacking" directed at the ATF. If the ATF wanted David Koresh, why hadn't they picked him up while he jogged out on the FM road? Why hadn't they arrested him when he went to gun shows in the area, to the Chelsea Street Pub in the mall, to the Lone Star Music and Sound Company to buy bigger and better speakers and electronic music equipment?

Everyone knew he had organized a rock band called Blind Wolfe that played in Dallas at a club called On The Rocks. He had gold cards printed up with "Messiah" on them. Beneath the single word he had printed "Cyrus Productions." On one corner was "David Koresh: Guitar, Vocals." On the other was "Steve Schneider: Music Manager."

Others remembered the Branch Davidians as working members of the community who had blue-collar jobs, nursing jobs, even white-collar jobs, while they contributed their salaries to support the communal living. They ran a farm and sold produce. Teachers were concerned about the children who attended school in nearby Axtell. They were missed by their classmates. As the days dragged on, Waco, as well as the rest of Texas and the United States, became more and more sympathetic to the cult and less and less sympathetic to the army camped on their grounds.

At the command of President Clinton, the FBI took control out of the hands of the disgraced ATF. When nothing happened and the siege dragged on, they began receiving the same bad press.

Of course, all was not well within the compound. Serious people began to have serious doubts about what they were doing when they saw the might of law enforcement arraigned against them. Some adults collected their children and came out. They were immediately arrested—a circumstance that did nothing to encourage others who might have felt like leaving. Probably many of those remaining felt they were caught between a rock and a hard place.

At the same time people from all over the United States as well as Australia were calling, concerned about their loved ones, particularly their girls, who were still inside the compound. The siege at Waco had gone international. It was the FBI who was between a rock and a hard place.

Meanwhile, a carnival atmosphere began to evolve on the little farm roads leading to the compound. Law enforcement brought in portable toilets, sandbags, and gasoline for a long siege. Sno-cone stands and signs appeared: "Is your church ATF approved?" and "R.I.P. the Bill of Rights" were just two. Reporters from the United Kingdom, Canada, and Australia set up their listening posts. As the number of people grew, so did the money Waco merchants were making on the debacle.

As public support grew stronger, lunch-hour demonstrations became common occurrences in Austin and Dallas. Hollywood agents showed up with checkbooks and contracts to sign made-for-TV movie deals.

Law enforcement's eyes were getting blacker. They strung razor wire around the perimeter and tried to keep the onlookers at a distance.

In the meantime Koresh made promises, then broke them. Of course, all this attention fed his ego enormously. As the Messiah to his flock, he now saw himself as able to control everyone outside the compound as well as in.

Then Koresh's mother hired attorney Dick Guerin, a smart Houston lawyer with a strong success record of defending important clients and getting them off. He was allowed inside on several occasions, but he stressed to the FBI that he was not a negotiator for them.

Finally, he brought news that his client would bring all his followers out as soon as they had observed Passover. "There is not going to be a violent end, at least as far as David is concerned."

This promise was made on the eve of Passover. On the night of Good Friday, Steve Schneider brought out a four-page, handwritten note dictated to Judy Schneider by David Koresh. There were dark references to being "devoured by fire."

Passover came and went, and the Davidians did not emerge. Guerin brought the information that David was writing a tract that he would give to his lawyer, and then they would all emerge.

On Monday morning, April 19, the chief negotiator told Steve Schneider that the government was through waiting. Armored vehicles were going to begin tearing chunks out of the building and pumping in tear gas.

Schneider interrupted the carefully prepared letter that was being read to him. "You're going to gas us?" he gasped. Immediately he clicked off the telephone, ripped the line from the wall, and chucked it out the window.

The FBI believed that Koresh wasn't likely to commit suicide or lead his followers in a mass self-destruction.

They were dead wrong.

The television cameras started rolling and the world caught the entire thing, including the confusion and the fires. In the end probably eighty-eight people died inside those flaming walls.

To this day the holocaust has not been forgotten.

William Sessions, the FBI chief, said the Davidians' response wasn't anticipated by the planners. Janet Reno apologized for approving the plan. "The buck stops with me," she said. Bill Clinton dodged and weaved when questioned. Finally, in the Rose Garden, he said, "I signed off on the general decision and [gave] her the authority to make the last call."

The eleven Davidians who came out on their own after the siege began or survived the fires were tried in Waco. After a six-week trial, the jury found them innocent, citing provocation by the ATF. As one juror reported, "I thought two agents in plain clothes should have gone in there and knocked on the door."

The tragedy of Ranch Apocalypse will fade with time as all Texas tragedies do. FBI profilers, seemingly blind to the climate in a state that prides itself on its rebellious attitude, "decided that there was little chance that David Koresh intended suicide." They paid no attention to his messages, the devotion of his followers, or the fact that he, along with the rest of Texas, remembered the Alamo!

No information can be discovered as to whether the government had heard before the tragedy that he had showed children how to put the barrel of a gun in their mouths and told them that it might someday be necessary for them to commit suicide.

David Koresh was no saint, even though he claimed to be Christ. Trapped by his own power, he kept testing his people, pushing them farther and farther. Abusing them, denying them sleep, denying them food, separating them from their loved ones, abusing their children.

Because they were his disciples, they allowed him to commit these outrageous acts. Without realizing what was happening to them, they became trapped in a symbiotic relationship. They needed to endure to prepare for heaven. He needed to demand that they endure more and more so they would obey him without question.

In the end, he demanded the destruction of them all.

One final word remains.

Although several men and women became totally disenchanted with the leader at Waco, they agonized for years afterward about their decision, wondering endlessly if they had damned their immortal souls. Even when they watched their friends and fellow worshipers burned to death, they still felt loss and uncertainty. Some of them underwent long periods of counseling. The families of others hired cult deprogrammers to help their relatives return to a more normal society.

Such is the power of the human need for belief in more than themselves.

"The Conversation"

(Sprightly tune, sung by two voices)

"Now, Janet, you must give me
Good reasons why I should
Launch a raid on Mt. Carmel
Where folks are doin' good?
There's something about religion.
I read it once one night.
It's in the Constitution
Or in the Bill of Rights."

"Oh, Bill, that man in Waco
Has wives and girlfriends too.
You'll look good by comparison.
Please let me push it through.
I'm your Attorney General,
I need to show my stuff.
The cops 'round here make fun of me.
It's time I showed I'm tough.

Don't sweat the Constitution.
No one's read it anyway.
It's a day for an auto-da-fé!"

"But, Janet, they've got weapons,
And someone might get shot.
I didn't serve in the army.
A soldier's what I'm not."
"Now, Bill, you won't be injured.
You stay here in D. C.
I'll send a group to handle it.
How about the F. A. T.?"

"That's ATF, Janet."

"Oh! Sorry."

"It's the Spanish Inquisition, Janet.
I don't think that I should.

Suppose I get compared to them.
You know that won't be good.
These folks just might be voters.
You might tromp on their rights.
I've got enough of troubles
Without starting any fights."

"Now, Bill, you know that Texans
Speak Spanish just for fun.
They won't think a thing about it
Unless you take their guns.
They'll think the tanks a'comin'
Are a football overtime.
Just turn me loose to get 'em,
And you'll see your numbers climb."

"Numbers climb, Janet?"

"Out the top, Bill!"

Together:

"Forget about the Bill of Rights.
They just get in the way.
It's a day for an auto-da-fé!"

"Yes! Don't sweat the Constitution.
No one's read it anyway.
What a day for an auto-da-fé!"

Note: An auto-da-fé (or burning at the stake) was the favorite method of punishing religious heretics during the Spanish Inquisition.

6

WHILE THEY SLEPT

Lightning flashed and streaked across the skies. Thunder boomed and reverberated along the Olmos Creek north and west of San Antonio. Thirteen inches of rain, a downpour never seen before, fell in the hills. The water rushed down the slopes into the narrow channel of the rockbound creek. It filled and turned into a torrent that spilled into the San Pedro and Alazan creeks, small tributaries of the San Antonio River. Muddy water began to move, gaining strength and height and depth as it coursed across the plain.

According to the *San Antonio Evening News* report for Friday, September 9, 1921, four and a quarter inches of rain fell between seven and midnight.

No one worried. No one was concerned unless his roof leaked. The placid river might rise an inch or two, but it would all wash on by morning. Their electric lights flickering and blinking with each flash of lightning, the citizens turned them out and climbed into their beds. Their houses were warm and comfortable. By morning things would begin to dry out.

Along the northern, scenic part of the river, chosen for its rocky heights above the water's edge, sat the city's pride, Brackenridge Park and Zoo. The rain coursing down the rocks added speed and depth to the river. Past the park it overflowed its banks. Two feet deep, it rolled down River Avenue.

Unheeded, it gathered strength and volume as it raced toward the Gulf two hundred miles away. It rampaged against the wooden bridges and walkways, setting them to swaying and creaking. It splashed and foamed against the concrete bridges built to handle the weight of motorcars. Debris of all sorts thudded against the supports and abutments.

Pile-up of debris against the bridge. Author collection.

But at about 10:00 P.M. in the blackness of the night, hundreds of men, women, and children were awakened to a wall of water crashing into their houses. As almost always occurs, the people who were least prepared to lose their homes lost them in a surge akin to Noah's flood. The Mexican communities alongside Alazan, Martinez, and San Pedro creeks were swiftly overwhelmed. Electric light poles toppled. Their live wires tossed and struck sparks in the mêlée.

One man escaped from his home when the water ran over his floor. Sensing it was a prelude to disaster, he started out into the storm. Only by clinging to trees, fences, the sides of buildings, and floating wreckage was he able to make his way to higher ground.

"It was impossible to stand on your feet against the current," he reported.

Then the river crested. One of nature's deadliest forces was unleashed—the power of a rampaging river ten to twenty feet above its banks. A wall of water topped by a roiling crown of white foam bearing limbs, small trees, lumber, railroad ties, and unidentifiable detritus broke from the banks and spread over an area two miles wide.

With the roar of the water came the crunches, scrapes, bangs, and thuds of cars and boats swept into bridges. Concrete and steel, tested to bear thousands of pounds of load, ripped apart. Glass smashed as the flood raced on, picking up houses. Floating, swirling, they encountered the sturdy water oaks and the tall cottonwoods, *los alamos,* for which the famous mission was named. There, like so much kindling, the houses broke apart against the trunks. Clapboarding, framing, studs, and shingles ripped loose and spun on like clubs through the murderous water.

In absolute darkness except for the occasional lightning flash, the screams of women and children could be heard above the roar. Cries for help echoed through the night to cease abruptly in mid-shriek.

Almost immediately, men began to attempt rescues. In many cases they found they could not stand in the water. They, too, were swept away or were forced back to higher ground to watch in helpless horror as an old man was dragged out of sight, as a screaming woman tried to climb out of a window with a baby in her arms. They watched and listened in anguish as a house disintegrated before their eyes while terrified shrieks issued from it.

Into the heart of San Antonio, the flood raced. Commerce and Houston streets, the two main corridors of downtown, ran parallel across the torrent. Pushed from its banks, the river lapped against Wolfe and Marx Department Store, ran into its basement, tossed pieces of wreckage against its huge store windows. They crashed in a shower of glass. Merchandise flowed out on a tide of oily water.

The clerks at the magnificent Gunter Hotel escaped to the mezzanine with the water lapping at their heels. Into the sanctuary of St. Mary's church, the water poured, tearing up the pews, overwhelming the chancel rails and the altar with its sacred objects, beating against the walls, and undermining the structure.

According to reporting from the *San Antonio Express,* water began flowing down St. Mary's Street at midnight. At midnight the army arrived in trucks with pontoons to rescue people in two-story buildings and be ready to prevent looting. At 12:20 College Street was flooded as far east as Navarro. Ten minutes more and the water was sloshing against the bottom of Navarro Street Bridge. At 12:45 it had risen to flow along both Navarro and Crockett streets.

At 1:00 A.M. electricity went down all over the city. Rushing water, laden with mud, rocks, and brush, added uprooted trees and telephone poles to the murderous mix. Unable to work at their presses any longer, reporters and pressmen found they had waited too long. They couldn't leave the building in safety. Water rushed in over the floor. It eventually rose a foot

St. Mary's Street at Travis. Author collection.

Debris threatens to sweep away the Navarro Street Bridge. Author collection.

deep. Within another forty-five minutes, the best estimates record it as five to six feet deep on Crockett and eight feet deep at Houston and St. Mary's.

At 2:00 A.M. the telephones went out. In essence the city was trying to operate deaf and blind.

In the absolute darkness and confusion, the water rushed in from the back of the Majestic Theater. It crossed the stage, destroying all the stage properties and lighting facilities before sweeping down into the orchestra pit and flooding the house with its velvet seats and curtains. Unbelievably, it rose high enough that the gilded rococo friezes around the proscenium arch and across the fronts of the boxes and balcony were flooded as well.

The Empire Theater, equipped with the expensive new projector and screen to show movies, as well as the home of one of the most important legitimate theater companies in the state, was a total wreck. Countless other buildings and their contents were badly damaged or destroyed so that repair would be more costly than simply replacing them. A considerable amount of the city's treasure was lost, and many businesses simply did not recover.

The *San Antonio Light* took a wild guess to estimate that as much as $5 million worth of damage had been done to the city and the area around it. Impossible to measure was the amount of San Antonio history and tradition being swept away.

"Where's the baby? Find the baby," a woman screamed. Policemen and firemen trying to organize themselves into some sort of teams heard her, but in the darkness could not find her or her baby. When she was later rescued after clinging to a tree, badly scratched, bruised, and shocked, she reported that her baby girl had been ripped from her arms though she'd lashed her to her chest. Her husband was never found.

Police themselves were hampered when their precinct building on Military and Main was flooded. The central police headquarters was like a wading pool, though the main floor was four feet about street level. Several hundred people spent the night in city hall.

Police reports were very pessimistic about survivors. "We saw people within twenty-five feet of us, yet [we were] unable to reach them."

Still, people went round in boats and found many to rescue. One woman sat on the roof of her house for three hours, calling for help in the darkness while twelve feet of water rose in her yard. Everything in her house was ruined, but she was rescued before the water receded.

Another man was swept out of his house away from his family. He struggled against the water to get back to them, but he kept getting pushed on downstream. An hour later, despairing, clinging to wreckage, he was washed toward a house lodged against the railing of the New Roman Street Bridge almost outside the city limits. He heard cries from inside. Climbing on top of it, he broke through the roof and found his wife and child floating on a mattress within one foot of the ceiling.

A traffic officer rescued three persons from the flooded district around 10:45 P.M. He hurried into the home of his neighbor, an elderly invalid, and carried her to safety. He helped another woman and her child into a tree because the water was rising so fast he didn't think he dared assist them any farther.

He dashed back to his own street in time to see his wife and three other women who had come to their house for refuge wading to safety through shoulder-high water and carrying their children on their backs. He dived in and swam to rescue his wife. As he reached her side, they turned to see their home swept away.

Like a scene from a dime novel or a silent movie, the best help arrived from Fort Sam Houston to the north. A cavalry unit came galloping in. It was aid the citizens of San Antonio must have welcomed as saviors from the past. The troopers heard occasional cheers as they deployed their mounts along the water's edge and spurred them into the flood to rescue women and children.

Heartening each other, police, soldiers, and cavalry worked together throughout the rest of the night lighted by flashlights, then kerosene lanterns, and last by motorcar headlights and spotlights.

At about two o'clock the water levels began to lower. The floodwaters raced on toward the Gulf. The people raised their heads and tried to make some sense of the nightmare that they had just endured. The swiftness of it stunned them. The destruction left them in awe.

At dawn the church bells began to ring.

In Texas, a state traditionally in need of rain, such a disaster was unprecedented. Even the two floods of the past two decades on the San Antonio River had been as nothing in comparison. People had shrugged, cleaned up the mud, and gone on with their lives.

How different this all was! San Antonio de Bexar, the state's oldest city, had been brought to its knees by its own aortic artery. Before expressways and turnpikes came into being, it was the pride and joy of her transportation system.

The city called itself the Venice of Texas because the ordinarily quiet San Antonio River meandered through its downtown area. Bridges for both pedestrian and vehicular traffic crossed and recrossed it. Cottonwoods and water oaks shaded it. Lovers strolled along beside it. Rowboats moved up and down it selling their handcrafted wares. Mariachis serenaded from its banks.

The long and colorful history of the city itself lined it. Fortunately, the Spanish missionaries had long been acquainted with the acts of God. To draw their water from the river in colonial times, the *padres* had used a Roman invention, the aqueduct. The four glorious Spanish missions, Concepción, Espada, Capistrano, and San José, had been built some distance from the river itself. The presidio called Alamo, where Texans fought to the last man and died to live in glory, stood less than a mile away but on a rise in the land.

Unfortunately, as the river became more popular, the unwary populace had lined it with grand hotels and hospitals, the city hall and the police station, St. Mary's Church and department stores that carried the finest goods to be bought on the continent. The fire department and the telephone exchange operated on streets that ran along beside it.

How could their river turn against them?

A four-page extra the *San Antonio Light* managed to publish on Saturday afternoon carried the following three-line headline:

37 Bodies Found; Dead May Total 200
Property Loss Estimated 5 Millions
Relief Work Proceeds at Rapid Pace

During the twentieth century, floods were the number-one natural disaster in the United States. No other type of disaster costs more lives or destroys more property. These terrible statistics result because only so many things can be done to take precautions. Everything depends on the one thing that no one has been able to control: the weather.

The U.S. Geological Survey categorizes floods into six different groups: regional; flash; ice jam; storm surge; dam and levee failures; and debris, landslide, and mudflow.

Flash floods are by far the most devastating of the six. Because they are so swift and sudden, people cannot get out of the way. Like the almighty wrath of God, they sweep all before them in minutes. Although they can last only a few hours, as in the case of San Antonio, their effects may be seen for months and felt for years.

In a river that winds between acres of asphalt and concrete, tall buildings and closely packed houses, they are particularly deadly. The people are grouped together more or less within easy reach. The concrete sidewalks and asphalt streets and parking lots do not absorb the water. The slate, tile, and shingle roofs as well dump it onto the streets and into the already swollen river. Even the storm drains empty into the river. When its banks are full, it has no choice but to rise higher and faster with each passing moment.

An abnormal amount of rainfall from a slow-moving thunderstorm can fill a small river like the San Antonio in a few hours. Its tributary streams, like the San Pedro, Martinez, and Alazan, fill also and flow into it. Given the absolute certainty that rivers flow downhill and gather strength as they flow toward their mouths, the reports of flood crests from ten to thirty feet high were probably not exaggerated.

Another tragic truth about flash floods is that almost half the deaths are in vehicles. The fact that most citizens of San Antonio were asleep in their beds rather than out driving probably accounts for the relatively low numbers of victims.

A present-day Ford Taurus weighs about thirty-five hundred pounds; a Ford Model-T of 1921 probably weighed no more than fifteen hundred. An unknowledgeable driver with no notion of the strength or depth of the water attempts to drive through. The water rises to the axles. One foot of water exerts five hundred pounds of force. Two feet of water has a buoyancy of fifteen hundred pounds plus one thousand pounds of force against the side of the car. Rising under the chassis, it floats the vehicle, be it a Taurus or Model-T.

Struggle as the driver might, his attempts to steer are futile. He has lost control. Within seconds, he's off the roadway and into the creek or river. The force of the rushing water strikes him broadside, rolls him upside down, and traps him and his passengers, perhaps his wife and children, inside. The windows are up because of the rain. The car's electrical elements short out. He cannot open the doors until the pressure inside is equal to the pressure outside—in other words, until the water has risen to the roof or floor of his car. He drowns in the darkness.

The citizens of San Antonio who emerged from the darkness after what must have seemed like the longest night of their lives were confounded by what they found. In the words of an uncredited *San Antonio Light* reporter, "The area was so intense and the number of workers so pitifully small for the job in hand that much of the tragic scene will never be recorded. There is none left to tell."

The morning after the catastrophic flood brought more sobering news.

The drinking water was immediately declared to be polluted. The gas substation on Matamoros Street had been struck by lightning, and gas mains all over downtown were under water. The electricity was out all over the city. Fortunately, a few businesses and hospitals had gasoline generators.

Virtually all areas of the city were at a standstill. Electric trolleys, the principal means of public transportation, stood useless in their barns and at the ends of track. Had the trolleys been operating, neither they nor motorcars nor trucks would have been able to negotiate the debris-clogged streets. The work force of the central city had no way to get to work except to wade or row in. The silt line on the walls of the buildings was six feet above the sidewalks.

The San Antonio Express reported on Sunday morning, September 11, thirty-nine dead and twenty missing. *The Light* reported thirty-eight bodies found. The discrepancies between the city's two sources of news reflected Saturday's chaos.

Even the railroads could not run. The tracks were clogged with debris in the underpasses and in some cases completely washed out. The southern end of the International and Great Northern Railroad trestles that spanned Alazan Creek near San Fernando cemetery had broken. Fifty feet of wreckage and debris had piled up against them.

The poorly constructed houses had been homes to the town's poorest

The trains stopped running also. Author collection.

people, mostly Mexican by descent. The wreckage, along with the bodies of their dogs, chickens, rabbits, geese, and other animals, littered the bed of the creek and piled up against the trestle. In silence the people gathered up what they could, threw clothing and bedclothes over hastily strung lines to dry, and began to bring in a bit of dried wood to start fires over which to boil water and to cook.

Worst of all, the temperature range that day was between eighty-six and ninety with more rain forecasted. It was going to be a day in hell as corpses and rotting vegetation quickly began to putrefy. Stations opened all over the city for people to come and get fresh, safe water. Water wagons drove down into the hard hit areas, and people lined up with whatever they could find to store it in.

Harbingers of horrors to come were the bodies of three children found almost immediately. A five-year-old Mexican boy was found lodged in the top of a tree in the river bottom west of St. John's Orphanage. Two more bodies of little girls were recovered an hour later, one lodged in debris and the other face down in the bed of a stream near the steelworks.

Every business had sustained damage and would be operating, if at all, under straitened conditions. Baylor Hospital had moved all its patients and personnel to the second floor when the water submerged the first. The cleanup effort would take days to render the floors, walls, and furniture sanitary for easily infected patients.

Still, all the Methodist churches in the downtown area announced that services would be held at 9:15 on Sunday morning. Only St. Mary's Cathedral had been wrecked beyond salvaging. The Masons offered the Scottish Rite Cathedral farther up the same street to the parishioners. Few people cared to venture out, however.

Meanwhile, the rest of Texas was in no position to help. Indeed, if the Federal Emergency Management Agency program had been in existence in 1921, the towns and cities on the Brazos, San Marcos, Colorado, and San Antonio rivers would have qualified for immediate assistance as disaster areas.

Over eighteen inches of rain fell in the same twenty-four hours at Austin, a city built on hills rising above the Colorado River. Her streets were impassable in the low spots. No trains were running north or south out of the capital. San Marcos, on the highway between San Antonio and Austin, was mostly underwater.

In Cameron to the northeast, the Little River had overrun its banks and flooded hundred of acres of farmland, stripping away crops still in the field about to be harvested. Cattle herds and horses drowned. A tornado struck at midnight just north of the town.

The Rio Grande rose twelve feet at McAllen and Brownsville, but the levees were high and well maintained. It stayed within its banks.

True to human nature, disaster brings out the very worst in some people. The army had come in to prevent looting, but the scope of the flood was so widespread that they had little effect. The police and military began to issue passes to try to keep people out of the downtown area. By Saturday afternoon, several arrests had been made despite looters' protesting that they were in the area rescuing their belongings. As of six o'clock a curfew had been announced allowing no one into the area during the night.

Unfortunately, police officers had been on duty so long, in many cases all night Friday night, all day Saturday, and into Sunday, that they were not able to respond to the messages and complaints coming in from the area along Martinez and Alazan creeks. Help arrived Monday morning when one thousand to fifteen hundred soldiers came to relieve them. The fresh troops were stationed at every intersection and set to patrol the city streets.

Still, people were able to sneak through in the dark. By Sunday morning one civilian had been shot when he refused to stop and identify himself at the command of a soldier who had observed him carrying goods from a damaged house.

At about the same time, the Red Cross opened quarters for relief and began making arrangements to distribute food and donated clothing and to assign people places to stay if they had lost their homes. Girls with bits of red cloth pinned to their sleeves in the shape of crosses drove flivvers—lightweight, cheap automobiles—around the city streets collecting clothing and other household goods from donors.

The *Light* reported, "Mexicans welcomed their destitute friends and neighbors with the most beautiful generosity."

On Saturday, Mayor O. B. Black organized a citizens committee that promptly did what politicians do best. It asked for money for a fund of $25,000 to purchase food and clothing. On Monday morning the town had contributed nearly $18,000, and relief efforts were under way.

By that time the death toll had risen to forty-five, with twenty-two missing and twenty-nine injured seriously enough to require medical aid. The waters had receded. The city announced that water services had been restored, but the stream from faucets would be somewhat reduced.

The water commissioner reminded everyone that the water came from

Families along Alazan Creek help each other. Author collection.

artesian wells that had not been contaminated by the flood. However, everyone was urged to conserve water until the electric pumping system had a chance to build the water levels to city needs.

In the meantime, to get everyone to their jobs on Monday morning, many of the trolley car crews voluntarily ran their own autos over the lines to pick up their regular customers and let them off at their stops. Business resumed as usual. Stores and banks opened while in the background gasoline pumps chugged away, pumping oily water out of their basements to flow into the streets and down to the peaceful river, which had been out of its banks only a little under four hours.

The evening edition of the *San Antonio Light* reported $21,000 was available to needy families and predicted by nightfall that the full $25,000 would be given for immediate relief. It also cautioned citizens to give no money to solicitors going door to door. They were taking money under false pretenses and should be turned away.

Instead, everyone was asked to send donations directly to the Chamber. And they continued to pour in. An entire column in the paper listed the donors' names, including Diego Guevarra, who gave fifteen cents, and Josephine Valdez, who gave a dime. The Joske Brothers, who owned one of the big department stores, gave $1,000, and Central Christ Church gave $500.

People today can only marvel at the generosity and self-sufficiency of the city and its governing body. The *San Antonio Evening News* /*Price 2 Cents—Pay No More—Don't Be Held Up* on Monday evening, three days after the disaster, headlined, "CITY BECOMING NORMAL." According to the reporter, "RAPID PROGRESS IS MADE IN CLEANING UP STREETS," and more important, a bond issue was being written for the rehabilitation of the city and for building a protective dam at the base of Olmos Basin.

Schools were set to reopen Tuesday. Lights were promised for the evening. Efforts were redoubled to collect all the trash, debris, and garbage and to pump all remaining water from basements to prevent the spread of diseases. Places were designated where people could carry bodies for identification and embalming.

The soldiers remained in the city for a few more days to insure that no looting or violence would take place. In addition to acting as a deterrent, they had been invaluable in assisting in the cleanup. They had erected a tent city on the west side as temporary housing for Mexican families. They had also overseen the burning of the drowned bodies of pets and livestock.

Besides serving as the major disbursers of information, the newspapers carried story after story of incredible heroism, including that of two men staying in a downtown hotel. They had heard cries from a small house torn loose and foundering a block away. Although they were strangers, not even townsmen, they waded and eventually swam to aid a mother and five children, transferred them from the flooded house to the rooftop, and waited with them for the daylight, when they were rescued by boat.

Editorials and front-page exhortations began to appear in the papers drumming up civic pride. An enterprising reporter or editor wrote an oath and ran it on the front page: "I AM THE SPIRIT OF SAN ANTONIO." In part it says, "I will fight all the harder to make San Antonio the flower of the southwest, to bloom courageously . . . in the wreckage. . . . I will fight back. I will not give up."

Another newspaper exhorted the citizens, "You're not licked till you quit. Don't quit!"

Every paper until the end of the week was filled with stories about individual heroism side by side with notices of charitable donations from organizations, businesses, and individuals. Utility workers worked around the clock to get services on line. By this time the American Red Cross was everywhere, as were soldiers, national guardsmen, Texas Rangers, and other law enforcement agencies, to ensure that minimal looting occurred. The $25,000 in donations swelled to $50,000 by Tuesday.

In the meantime, the city's administration met and acted after a fashion. Mayor O. B. Black called the Chamber of Commerce for an $8 million appropriation to repair, replace, and renovate. The first $5 million would be to repair the damage to the downtown area. Half a million of that would go to repair the famous bridges and the streets that ran into them.

The rest would be available to replace the merchandise lost and damaged beyond salvaging by the force of the oily water. A survey conducted of businesses downtown found that only two carried flood insurance. Since these businesses were the basis of San Antonio's wealth and growth, the money was deemed well spent to restore them as quickly as possible.

The other $3 million was earmarked for the rebuilding of the houses west of the city, in particular those along the creeks. These belonged in many cases to the poorest of the poor, who could least afford to lose anything and had no means of restoring what they had. The newspaper account listed the dead by name, age, and address on the front page of the paper. In a subheadline it reported forty-five dead, twenty-two missing, twenty-nine injured, and scores homeless.

The mayor then promised to call for a bond issue to construct a dam at the base of the Olmos Basin seven miles west of San Antonio. He also reported that he had received letters and telegrams of sympathy from cities across the United States and from President Álvaro Obregón of Mexico. Many cities had offered aid, including Austin, Corpus Christi, Fort Worth, St. Louis, Dallas, and Waco. He announced that he had proudly declined their offers, saying that San Antonio could and would take care of its own.

With civic pride running high, the consensus was that he had taken the proper course of action. They could take care of their problems by themselves.

Wednesday's *San Antonio Evening News* proudly announced "TRAIN SERVICE BEING READJUSTED AGAIN." Although San Antonio's rail service had been reestablished through Austin, it could go no farther because of damage to tracks to the north. The farthest west of the major cities in Texas and the closest to the hill country and the panhandle plateau, San Antonio had been hit first and caught unawares. The other cities that had offered help had each been hit by a flood caused by the same wet front.

The full extent of the slow-moving rainstorms across Texas became known when Austin reported the crest of the Colorado had passed on into the Gulf while Houston was still waiting for the flood crest of the Brazos to pass through its metropolis. Because of what had happened in San Antonio, both cities, as well as smaller towns farther east and south, had been able to get their citizens out of the way and do some work on their levees.

Under the headline "LANE OF DEATH ACROSS STATE CAUSED BY FLOOD," one article reported that 175 bodies had been found across Texas. The paper further estimated that the death toll would probably reach two hundred fifty. The count included the forty-nine dead in San Antonio. The other cities had suffered fewer casualties. The largest number of lives lost elsewhere was mostly in rural areas where people living along the rivers were caught as unawares as San Antonio had been.

As the waters drained away, cool heads began to question what had happened. Gradually, accusing eyes turned toward the political class. By Sunday morning, September 18, just a week and a day after the flood, the *San Antonio Express* broke unsettling news in a front-page story complete with a photograph of a Catholic priest holding a sheaf of papers. Montaged in the same photograph were a Bible and an altar crucifix. For one of the holiest cities in Texas with a huge Catholic majority, the images instructed citizens to read the expose with great attention.

The gist was that consulting engineers had reported to the city nine months ago that the San Antonio River was unsafe. Her channel needed to be deepened by 50 percent and other improvements made. The cost was projected at $960,000, a mere fraction of the terrible property losses incurred during the flood. Nothing, of course, could replace the lives lost.

The paper also reported that the mayor had elected not to present this information to the city.

The hue and cry was loud and long. Mayor Black served out his term in ignominy. In the words of John B. Tobin, the man who was elected to take his place, "Black was washed out of office."

Still, nothing was done. The *Express* published a long editorial with flood pictures in November 1923, reminding citizens of what had happened to them and calling for a vote for passage of a $4.35-million bond package to build the dam. By that time the city had spread westward, and citizens in Alamo Heights screamed that their lives would be endangered because their backs would be to the dam, which could break at any moment. Their fears were allayed when they were assured that the amount of water retained behind the dam would never be so much as to pose a danger.

Still, nothing was done.

Another proposal was for the straightening of the city's famous Horseshoe Bend in the center of the Paseo del Rio, the Spanish name for the Riverwalk. Some people wanted to concrete over the land in the bend and use it for a gigantic parking lot. Those determined to keep as many of the original curves and bends as possible waged a campaign against that idea.

The San Antonio Conservation Society was formed in 1924. The bend remained. The entire project, including beautification, continued to be talked about until the San Antonio River Authority was established by the Texas legislature in 1937.

Even with the state of Texas behind the project, nothing was done until after a series of floods in September 1946 cost six lives and $2.1 million in property loss. In 1951 the Army Corps of Engineers completed its study and recommendations. The San Antonio Channel Improvement Project and the Escondido Creek Channelization Project were approved by the U.S. Congress in the Flood Control Act of September 3, 1954.

And so it goes! In 1968 for her two hundred fiftieth birthday, San Antonio built the Tower of the Americas along its banks. It also established the Institute of Texan Cultures, now part of the University of Texas. In 1976 more studies were made; more money was appropriated. Again in 1982, 1988, 1990, 1992, and so forth.

The project will never be completed, but many, many people will have made a great deal of money—perhaps as much as $100 million on a project that should have cost approximately $3 million if it had been done the first time around.

Nevertheless, the ongoing building and constructing and refurbishing

Navarro Street Bridge today above the Riverwalk. Author photo.

The Venice of Texas today on the Riverwalk. Author photo.

have produced one of the wonders of Texas, the United States, and the Western Hemisphere: twenty-one city blocks downtown with rock retaining walls, picturesque foot bridges, rock-surfaced walks, and landscaped banks. Every night of the week, the restaurants and shops are full. A huge shopping center has been built beside it. Elegant hotels and apartment buildings stretch their balconies above. San Antonio has embraced it. No other downtown in America can boast such a vibrant segment. People in San Antonio in a position to make money from construction seem assured of a gold mine into the twenty-first century as the Riverwalk extends farther and farther south.

The flood of 1921 can be said to be the end and the beginning of San Antonio as one of America's most welcoming cities.

"Stand Together"
(Fiddle tune with knitting needles keeping time on a dinner triangle)

Lightning tore them clouds to ribbons,
Their bellies opened up.
While thunder boomed, the rain came pelting down.
New-fangled e-lectricity flickered,
Then it quit!
So we climbed into bed all over town.

Next thing we heard the dog a-barking—
A most hellacious noise.
We rolled out and there was water everywhere.
My furniture was floating two foot deep.
I near cried.
And my wife yelped and hopped up on a chair.

That muddy San Antone had riz,
A-roaring like a train.
Come sailing by the window was my old Model-T—
We jumped up on the mattress and we floated
Outta there
Cause the whole durn town was headed for the sea.

Well, we roosted on the railroad bridge,
A bunch of half-drowned birds,
While we sadly watched our houses floating by.
But nobody come to help us, so we gotta
Help ourselves.
It was then we stood together do or die.

A Texas motto for the ages.
Stand together!
And we will, like we did at Sabine Pass and Alamo.
And if we come to troubles, we'll come round
On our own.
It's how we've lived and how we mean to grow.

In the dawn we joined together rich and poor,
Young and old.
We took no time to stand around and moan.
We cleaned it up and built it back
Good as new!
And it was better cause we'd done it on our own.

7

SKY-HIGH IN TEXAS CITY

Nearly 80 percent of Earth's air is composed of nitrogen, an almost inert gas. Only under extreme circumstances, such as a thunderstorm, does it combine with water to form compounds called nitrates, which are carried by rain down into the soil to enrich it.

So long as man was a primitive food-gatherer, the process worked perfectly. But as civilizations spread across the globe, the infusion of nitrates by thunderstorm became woefully insufficient. Once-fertile farmlands became deserts that had to be abandoned. By the beginning of the twentieth century, Thomas Malthus's dire predictions of mass starvation seemed inevitable unless scientists could increase food production.

Scientists sought to duplicate the work of the lightning to "fixate" practically inert nitrogen in a bond with other elements to create nitrates. In Germany, chemist Fritz Haber, the director of the Kaiser Wilhelm Institute, miraculously created a way of fixing the element. His process turned nitrogen and two extremely volatile, highly flammable gases, oxygen and hydrogen, into a white, granular fertilizer. The process became the wonder of the world. Incredibly, it could be produced for relatively low cost because it was quite literally made of air.

In 1918 he was awarded the Nobel Prize for Chemistry; his method was of "universal significance for the improvement of human nutrition." Ironically, his creation was also the most powerful and deadly explosive created until the advent of the atom bomb. Even now as the twentieth century has turned into the twenty-first, it has become the weapon of choice from Oklahoma City to Baghdad.

Five-hundred-pound bombs, two parts ammonium nitrate to one part

119

TNT, rained down on Germany and Japan during World War II. Even as that "hot" war ended, the Cold War with Russia cranked up. After years of war, Europe and Asia were vulnerable to the communists.

From Tokyo in 1946, General Douglas MacArthur demanded millions of tons of ammonium nitrate. "Either bread or bullets for the starving, defeated people," he told President Harry Truman. From the Pantex plant in Amarillo, millions of pounds of fertilizer in an inert yet potentially deadly form were produced and shipped to the docks at Houston.

Recognizing the danger, Houston made a decision that undoubtedly saved her industry and allowed her to grow to be the largest city in Texas. She ruled shortly after the shipments started that her port would no longer handle ammonium nitrate in any form. So the potentially dangerous substance was loaded on railway cars and hauled fifty miles down the road.

And that is why on April 10, 1947, two Liberty ships built in California during World War II were lying in the main slips at Texas City and a third was on her way to be steered into the north slip.

Lined up on either side of the wharf were a dozen industries, all handily located where the trains of the Texas City Terminal Railway Company ran on one side and the ships sailed on the other. Among them were the Monsanto Chemical plant and its offices, the S. W. Sugar and Molasses Company, the Sid Richardson Oil Company, the Republic Oil Company, the Humble Oil Company Tank Farm, as well as oil and propane gas storage tanks for various companies as far as the eye could see.

Down the channel from Houston came the ten-thousand-ton Liberty ship *Grandcamp,* a grand name for an ugly, wallowing vessel never built to last. One of a number of ships riveted and welded together in as little as forty-eight days, she carried thousands of tons of supplies and ammunition to American soldiers fighting in Germany. Given the constant torpedoing of her sisters by the U-boats, her chances of surviving her maiden voyage were slim. But survive she did. With that war won, she'd been sold to the French to do grunt work for the rest of her life.

So on April 14, there she was, wallowing slightly in Galveston Bay, her holds only partly filled with cotton, sisal twine, shelled peanuts, oil-well equipment, tobacco, and sixteen cases of Belgian small-arms ammunition that should have been taken off in Venezuela. And around her as she rode, the sky opened up with a noisy thunderstorm—rain, thunder and, of course, lightning.

The old Liberty ship Grandcamp. *After she exploded, all that remained of her was part of her anchor dredged from the bottom of the harbor. Courtesy of Moore Memorial Public Library, City of Texas City, Texas.*

Meanwhile, on the Texas City docks her last load was waiting for her—51,502 hundred-pound, six-ply, moisture-proof paper bags. Heat and humidity had begun their work. A few of the bags had already split open, spilling pellets of fertilizer on the dock. That wasn't all that was happening to the cargo. Longshoremen waiting in the chill at 6:00 A.M. discovered they could press their hands and bodies against the bags to keep warm. The bags were unnaturally hot. Some were literally scorching. The fertilizer was combusting spontaneously.

For three straight days the longshoremen loaded the ammonium nitrate into the No. 4 and No. 2 holds, already half full of other exports. On the morning of the third day, with twelve thousand bags still to be loaded, someone noticed the smell. Smoke trailed up at the middle point of No. 4 hold. From six, maybe seven, bags deep down in the stack against the hull of the ship, a yellow glow was visible. The six-ply paper was burning. No one was sure why the bags were burning. They contained only fertilizer.

Still, the captain had no cause for particular alarm. Even though No. 4 hold was directly against the fuel oil supply in the center of the ship, a fire in it would be easy to extinguish.

The French sailors and the longshoreman tried to put it out with a few fire extinguishers and some gallon jugs of water. Their efforts evaporated almost as fast as the water touched the stacks. Greenish-yellowish-orange smoke began rising out of the hold.

At 8:20 A.M. on April 16, Captain Charles de Guillebon sounded the emergency whistle, three short blasts and one long one. He ordered a tarp put over the hold and the pumps started. The idea was to starve the fire of oxygen at the same time they pumped in seawater from the wharf side. Whether he thought about what he might be pumping into the hold is unknown. Certainly, the water was thick with oil and chemical spills.

About that time someone remembered that No. 5 hold contained ammunition. Guillebon's order was, "Get it the hell off the ship."

At the same time, seven hundred fifty feet away in the Texas City Terminal Railway offices, Supervisor Mike Mikeska noticed the fire. It could be big trouble. Mikeska, the de facto boss of the harbor, took matters into his own hands. He called for two tugboats to report to Texas City. The tugboats got under way immediately.

Still, no one was too concerned about the fire. There were fires all the time along the docks. Out of curiosity, people gathered to watch the efforts to put it out.

Despite the millions of dollars' worth of industry within her city limits, Texas City was still a poor, backwater town. Few knew or cared that she had had to sell her fireboat for lack of funds. The fire department was made up of volunteers.

This same lack of money accounted for the fact that half the children in Texas City were not in school that morning because overcrowding had forced them to go in split shifts, a common phenomenon after World War II, when the birthrate skyrocketed. Close to half of these young children were in their homes, many in the area adjacent to the docks and the oil tanks. A few were lined up at a distance watching the action.

Many of those recognized Chief Henry Baumgartner of the Volunteer Fire Department. He checked in and began to make his plans. Quickly, he required six of his crew of volunteers to run a fifty-foot line of fire hose from pumps inside Warehouse O. Three pumps with 1,000-gallon capacity each tapped from an underground reservoir that held 277,000 gallons.

By that time it was 8:45 A.M.

At 9:01 the tarpaulin spread by Captain Guillebon caught fire from below. It rose like a paper bag caught by a whirlwind. The wooden planks laid across to anchor it tumbled away and thudded onto the deck. Guillebon ordered his men off the ship.

With steely determination Baumgartner led his men into the strange-colored smoke. Baumgartner's son Harold and two other boys had ridden down on their bikes to watch the excitement. The boy saw his father and twelve other men lower themselves through the hatches. Then, as now, the firemen hurried into the fire when others ran away. At the same time the water in Galveston Bay began to boil.

In Central High School the chemistry teacher, Mr. Rheems, had his class bunched at the second-floor window looking at the smoke swirling down Sixth Street. "What kind of nitrate could cause smoke to turn that color?" the teacher asked.

"If that wasn't a fire, that would be one of the prettiest things I've ever seen," Elaine Dupuy answered.

And the world exploded.

Just before he was knocked unconscious, one student saw a white object against the black smoke. It was the Piper Cub of World War II Marine Corps ace Johnny Norris. For ten dollars he'd taken a passenger up over the bay to see the show. The explosion ripped the wings upward off the plane, threw it up into the black smoke, and dropped its passengers in a corkscrew dive to their deaths west of the Monsanto plant.

At 9:12 A.M. a geologist in Denver, Colorado, monitoring his seismograph stared at the paper chart that recorded a spasm of such magnitude that he guessed it might have been an atomic bomb going off somewhere in Texas.

As *Grandcamp* disintegrated, chunks of her and her fourteen-million-pound cargo rained over the town, the harbor, the shrimp boats in Galveston Bay, and the roofs of the homes of the town's poorest families in El Barrio and the Bottom. Superheated pieces of metal—decks, screws, pistons, the anchor—bombed the oil tanks of Pan American, Sid Richardson, Amoco, Republic Refining, and Stone. The men at the petrochemical complex believed they were under attack. Twenty oil storage tanks were set ablaze.

In her death throes *Grandcamp* scooped out the entire basin. A twenty-foot tidal wave rose, containing not only seawater but diesel fuel, hydrochloric acid, ammonium nitrate, and styrene. On top of the wave was *The Longhorn II,* a one-hundred-fifty-foot-long, thirty-five-ton hydrochloric

Texas City ablaze. The choking smoke and flames would be blown by the gulf winds over the town towards Houston. Courtesy of Moore Memorial Public Library, City of Texas City, Texas.

acid barge. In accordance with the laws of physics, the tidal wave slapped the barge down on top of the dock and the smoking skeletons of the only three Texas City fire trucks. The force of the water destroyed the dockside café and dragged all the French sailors and the captain, as well as the others, out into the fiery water to their deaths.

Like the fires of hell, the dock and every piece of industry around it burst into flame. All the members of the fire department on the scene died instantly. In total twenty-seven firemen were never seen again. Their bodies were never recovered. It was the worst fire department tragedy of the twentieth century.

In Galveston across the bay, tall buildings constructed to withstand hurricane gale-force winds swayed. People ran into the streets thinking they were in the midst of an earthquake. Students at Galveston's Ball High School ran out into the park across the street, where everyone's clothing

Remains of the Texas City fire engine crushed by Longhorn II. *Her firemen, including the chief, were already dead. Courtesy of Moore Memorial Public Library, City of Texas City, Texas.*

became spattered as minute black dots of oil thrown sky high in an explosion like an atom bomb rained down upon their clothes and faces.

While Texas City lay almost paralyzed, its services unequal to the overwhelming task, Galveston mobilized. She was uniquely qualified to do so. For obvious reasons her hurricane and disaster plans were among the best in the world.

The county chairman of the Red Cross disaster medical aid committee had seen the explosion from his office window. He had immediately dispatched all the considerable facilities from St. Mary's Infirmary, the Marine Hospital, and the world-famous teaching hospital, John Sealy, where classes were instantly dismissed. The faculty, many of whom had served as military surgeons in World War II, organized themselves and their students into teams to triage the patients that would be arriving within minutes.

Within thirty minutes Galveston ambulances and city buses pulled off their regular routes congregated at the hospitals to pick up doctors, nurses, and fifty husky high school boys from Ball High School to act as stretcher bearers.

The convoy moved swiftly, unimpeded by traffic as self-appointed traffic wardens took up positions and stopped vehicles from crossing the four-lane highway leading to the causeway. This convoy and a contingent of almost fifty vehicles from Fort Crockett, the local army base, formed part of a steady stream of ambulances, fire trucks, taxis, heavy construction equipment, buses, military vehicles, and private cars to aid the stricken city. Within an hour of the *Grandcamp*'s explosion, the first vehicles began to arrive.

The situation south of 8th Street in Texas City was grave and getting graver by the minute. The unprecedented number of seriously injured people staggered the imagination, as did the wounds they had sustained. In addition to concussions, fractured skulls, broken bones, partially amputated limbs, and loss of blood, the clothing of many victims had been blown off their bodies by the blast. Their exposed skin had been coated with everything stored in the giant tanks that completely surrounded the slips. Crude oil, fuel oil, molasses, sulfur, hydrochloric acid, benzol, and a dozen other substances had come pouring out of broken pipes, storage tanks, and warehouses all along the water front.

Since they were recognizable as human beings only by the general shape of their bodies, none of the emergency personnel could tell whether they were black, Mexican, or white. Emergency care was delivered on a first in, first out basis.

In the meantime, the site of the explosion was a picture of hell itself. When the few survivors around the dock managed to make their way out of the wreckage of their buildings, they had to wade through pools of chemical-laced water with red-orange flames dancing on top of the ripples. As they got farther from the blast sight, those who could ran for their lives. Many did not even realize that they were naked, their clothes blown or burned off, their bodies scorched black, their skin permeated with a black substance later discovered to be a combination of oil and molasses from the S. W. Sugar and Molasses Company, which had disintegrated in the explosion. Their open wounds were contaminated with dirt, sand, and oyster shell, as well as shards of wood, metal, and glass.

At the city hall at the adjunct of 6th Avenue and 6th Street, six thousand feet away but well within the range of the devastated area, Chief of Police William Ladish watched the smoke rise from the docks. At the time of the explosion, he had been slammed to the floor, glass from the shattered window cutting his face and hands. He and the dispatcher discovered that the police radio had been knocked out. Through the glass-littered streets, Ladish ran to the telephone exchange where he called the Houston Police Department, requesting fifty officers and all available ambulances.

The calls had already begun to go out, some from telephone company supervisors who had instructed operators to alert all available hospitals and police departments. Like the personnel at John Sealy Hospital in Galveston, the National Guard in Houston had already gone into action.

Meanwhile the calls went out over the radios all across Texas. From El Paso to Amarillo to Brownsville at the mouth of the Rio Grande, ambulances, medical teams, and fire trucks were dispatched. The assistant fire chief, who had been out of town, returned immediately to find that he had no equipment and only half the crew. They could do little more than direct traffic for the men riding in from other towns.

In the wreckage that had been the industries of the town, people began to take stock and take command. Used to handling emergency situations with highly volatile products, employees from Carbide and Carbon Chemical Company, Pan American Oil, and Sid Richardson Refinery had formed rescue teams and sent their company firefighters and emergency equipment dockside.

They found the damage overwhelming. The mission was, first, to pull people from the wreckage and get them to safety and, second, to put out the fires blazing everywhere before they caught more of the highly flammable liquids on fire.

Where to take the hundreds of injured became another problem. Texas City had only three clinics and ten doctors. Their facilities were small and ill staffed. They had also suffered damage, as had everything else in the city, from the force of the explosion and flying glass. Moreover, they were without water, electricity, and gas because all city services had been knocked out. Little could be done for the flood of patients beyond triage.

One merchant heard that children in all the schools, as well as in their homes, had been cut by flying glass. He ran into a pharmacy seeking medical supplies. With a companion and the permission of the pharmacist, they scooped up the stock lying on the floor and set up a first aid station for children in a vacant lot. Other merchants gave away their stocks of blankets and bedding.

Meanwhile, down at the docks the business of finding the living and the dead in the debris was a frightening and dangerous task. In the Monsanto plant, rescuers waded through oily water to their knees. Meanwhile, sulfur

*The massive cleanup. No city surviving an air raid could have been in worse condition.
Courtesy of Moore Memorial Public Library, City of Texas City, Texas.*

caught fire in Warehouse A. It ignited jute bagging and cotton bales, fueled by the oil spewing from broken pipes leading to the tank farms. The heat from flaming tanks of benzol, propane, and ethyl benzol melted the steel supports of the buildings, causing them to collapse and killing people who had taken temporary shelter inside. Captain Glen Rose of the Texas Highway Patrol tried to reach employees in the Monsanto complex but was only able to get close enough to hear their screams as they burned to death.

The twin problems of getting workers in and victims out were exacerbated by the wreckage lying atop the single shell-topped road leading down from the highway to the north slip and turning right to the main and south slips. There was simply no way to get emergency equipment into the devastated area.

Aboard *High Flyer,* in the main slip, six hundred feet from the spot where *Grandcamp* caught fire, Captain Mosley Petermann had seen the rising smoke. He had sounded the emergency alarm and scrambled all his men to their fire battle stations. He had closed all his hatches and ordered them sealed, including the hold that contained 961 tons of ammonium nitrate. He was considering getting his ship under way.

Too late! When *Grandcamp* went up, *High Flyer* was ripped from her moorings. Despite her two-ton anchor chain, she was driven sideways into the hull of another Liberty ship, *Wilson B. Keene,* also taking in cargo.

Gamely, Captain Petermann ordered the anchor lifted and the engines started to set his damaged ship out to sea, but the windlass had been destroyed by the force of the explosion that ripped the anchor out of the harbor bottom. Forty-eight minutes later, Petermann ordered his crew to abandon ship. They leaped onto the deck of *Wilson B. Keene,* ran across her deck, and scrambled down rope ladders into the flaming wreckage and yellow chemical clouds on the dock.

The dense, black smoke, the flame, the poisonous gases kept the tugs and buoy tenders from Galveston, as well as the Coast Guard, from drawing too close to the docks. Like a time bomb, *High Flyer* waited, her hull growing ever hotter.

At this point Hal Boyle, a World War II frontline correspondent filed his firsthand account: "I have seen no concentrated devastation so utter, except in Nagasaki, Japan, victim of the second atom bomb."

The Bay Towing Company in Galveston called together the crews of its four tugs. They were told that at least eight hundred tons of ammonium nitrate were aboard *High Flyer.* She was thought be on fire. Then the cap-

High Flyer's *propeller stands like a bastion at the gates to the harbor today. So heavily damaged by the explosion that she could not be moved, she herself exploded. Author photo.*

tains called for volunteers. One by one, hands went up until all four crews were ready.

Under a sky black as the inside of a coffin, the moon and stars obscured behind the billowing smoke, northwest winds blowing in their faces, the crews of *Guyton, Albatross, Clark,* and *Miraflores* chugged past Bolivar Peninsula toward the smoking, flaming wreckage of Texas City.

Within minutes they began to encounter floating debris. To their horror, among the flotsam they saw floating bodies. Almost two hours were required to make the trip. At 10:00 p.m. *Albatross* spotted *High Flyer* wedged against her sister ship. She was not what the crews expected to find.

The old Liberty ship looked like a neon-red fireworks display, thousands of sparks firing in columns out of her holds, highlighting the billowing mustard-yellow smoke. The four million pounds of raw sulfur stored next to the fuel oil were on fire. Beyond that, the ammonium nitrate smoldered.

Whether the dock still stood, the crew could not tell. Timbers slapped against the tug's hulls. Pieces of jagged, glowing metal stuck straight out of the water. It was a scene scraped out of hell itself.

Guyton and *Albatross* made the first approach. The first tug tried to run a hook through *Flyer*'s anchor chain. The task was daunting, because yellow sulfurous gas cut visibility down to a few yards. Fortunately, the sailors had gas masks. Once the hook line was attached, *Guyton* tried to back off, but the line snapped and ricocheted like a bullwhip.

High Flyer was embedded into *Wilson B. Keene*. Daring instant death, *Albatross* pulled alongside. Sailors from both vessels scrambled over the ship, trying to cut her free, trying to drag her off. Finally, they thought they had succeeded. She moved fifty feet down the slip, then stopped as if locked in place. To their horror, despite their best efforts, she seemed to be settling, dragging them back toward her by their own towlines.

Somebody yelled to cut the lines, but Petermann belayed that order. Some of *Guyton*'s men were still on board the doomed ship. Refusing to abandon his crew, the captain bravely steered the tug back alongside. His men jumped and shimmied down the bowlines. Then Petermann gave the order to get the hell away. He followed the other tugs for the safety of Galveston Bay. They were only six hundred feet out when the inferno behind them melted the bulkheads.

At 1:10 A.M. on Thursday morning, April 17, a three-thousand-foot tower of fire from *High Flyer* spouted upward into the darkness. The Gulf of Mexico came alight. The brilliant tower revealed the devastation of what was once Texas City.

Only a year and a half before, the United States had been at war with Japan and Germany. The ports around the Houston–Galveston–New Orleans triangle had been on constant alert with disaster plans and drills. The people of the cities to a certain extent had honed their skills to handle themselves in an emergency.

This training clicked into place. Like children lining up for a fire drill, more often than not people did their jobs, without hesitation. In another time and another place, many more victims and much more destruction might have occurred. Medical assistance was as good as or better than could be expected. In a town built on a spit of land with only one highway and two other narrow roads leading into it, access was handled by the army and state troopers who assumed their posts within hours. Finally, civil peace was maintained. Very little looting or lawlessness occurred.

Still, the devastation shocked the nation. America had never seen a town "bombed" before.

The aftermath was almost as shocking as the event. Fourth Army epidemiologists suggested that a plague might be imminent. Bodies were rapidly decomposing in the steamy heat generated by the blasts. Hundreds were

Texas City after most of the smoke had cleared. Courtesy of Moore Memorial Public Library, City of Texas City, Texas.

not found immediately. Some were never found. Dead animals and schools of dead fish added to the odorous mix. The explosion had unleashed armies of rats and snakes that had scurried, slithered, and swum for their lives from their destroyed homes. Cockroaches, primary spreaders of disease, were rousted from the dark. In the homes still standing all across Texas City, food rotted in pantries, in refrigerators, and on kitchen tables. Sewer pipes had smashed, exposing their contents. Mosquitoes, the scourge of the Gulf Coast, came in hordes.

In an effort to combat the roaches and mosquitoes, the entire city was sprayed extensively over a period of several weeks with DDT. Twenty-five years later the chemical was banned after extensive toxicological studies revealed that it persisted up to fifteen years in the environment, where it was shown to lead to virulent cancers with tumors affecting the nervous system, the kidneys, the liver, and the reproductive organs.

For the last half of the twentieth century, graveyard humorists jokingly referred to Texas City as "Toxic City."

Exemplifying what all the citizens of Texas City felt after enduring the explosions, the pollution of their environment, and the staggering loss of life was the reaction of a pipe fitter from the Carbide plant. Prey to feelings of utter helplessness, of delayed shock, and of unmitigated agony of body and soul, he broke down and cried to John Hill, a chemical engineer, who had labored without ceasing at the side of Mayor Curtis Trahan. For forty straight hours, the pipe fitter had worked as a volunteer embalmer inside McGar's garage across the street from the high school. He was holding his own, numbing his mind to the horror, operating on the edge, until he finally had dropped in his tracks.

When other workers pulled him aside and gave him the once-over, they found that his feet and legs had become swollen grotesquely from standing so long. In an effort to relieve him, they had had to cut off his prized cowboy boots.

He, who had been able to sustain himself through inhuman stress, suddenly went over the edge. A strong and gallant man wept as if his heart were broken.

All around him, the other citizens of Texas City were clearly sitting on the edge.

Aid came first at the behest of the biggest gangster on the Texas Gulf Coast. Sam Maceo was involved in everything that went on in Galveston. Mafia connected, he "imported" booze from Mexico during Prohibition. Indeed, he supplied the entire state. He had never been truly accepted in the elite and distinctly snobbish old city, not so very long ago the biggest in Texas. He was wealthy, but so were many others.

He took his chance to shine for the good of a sister city and in so doing to polish his reputation in that part of Texas. He imported Hollywood movie stars to perform for charity. If they couldn't come, they were bullied into sending a sizable check. Frank Sinatra, a personal friend, was already on board for all things Italian. Maceo called another old friend, Phil Harris. Phil could bring his wife, Alice Faye, along with Jack Benny, Gene Autry, George Burns, and Gracie Allen. Together they planned a big benefit for the end of the month, by then only ten days away.

Their star-spangled efforts were not the only ones. Eventually private donations reached $1.063 million, an enormous sum in 1947 when $100 a month was a handsome salary.

Of course, the money raised only amounted to a drop in the bucket. The official number of identified dead rose to 405. The number listed as missing was 113, but so many people living in the Mexican Barrio and the Bottom, where the black folk lived, were recorded nowhere in America or on earth. Those two areas, scheduled for development, had been wiped out.

Likewise, the bodies of children were especially difficult to locate. Burned, blown apart, crushed under debris, their very existence was gone if their parents were also killed. Sixty-three bodies were so badly damaged that no one could identify what was left. The total official number was placed at 581.

The damage to the social fabric and the infrastructure of the town, not to speak of the damage to homes, schools, businesses, and churches, was incalculable. Many people in Texas City came to believe that some men and women had discovered the perfect moment to leave behind their jobs, their families, and everything else that had become a burden in their lives. In a word, they disappeared.

Plans to bury the unidentified dead hit a snag when a proposal was made to a small town west of Texas City. When a representative approached the city council, they were asked a strange question. "Are there blacks that you are going to bury?"

When the answer was yes, they refused to sell the land. "Blacks have never been buried alongside whites, and they never will be."

That blacks had labored beside whites and died beside them was never considered. The attitude was a reflection of the pitiless prejudice of the times.

Exactly a year to the day after *Grandcamp* exploded, Civil Action 787 was brought against the "United States of America, Defendant." It was the first time that the government of the United States had ever been sued. The understanding had always been that the government was entitled to sovereign immunity. In other words, the king could do no wrong.

But Congress had recently passed a sweeping restructuring of the American government. The Federal Tort Claims Act was a part of it. It stated that the U.S. government could be held accountable for its actions. In effect, it said that the king could be judged by his people.

In thirty-three pages, the civil action listed seventy-three plaintiffs led by Elizabeth Dalehite, the widow of a sea captain whose body had been decapitated when he had gone into the smoke to aid the stricken ship's crew.

The document accused the government of willful negligence when it "sold and shipped large quantities" of ammonium nitrate to Texas City without saying that the chemical compound was inherently dangerous. Therefore, each of the plaintiffs had suffered grievous loss "caused by the negligence of the defendant."

Nothing was done immediately. Indeed, proceedings were delayed until two years later, April 1949. By that time the desperation of the hundreds of widows, widowers, sons, daughters, grandparents, and cousins had intensified. They had been left with their creditors calling, their homes destroyed, their insurance policies in their homes destroyed as well, their medical bills unpaid with no hopes of paying, their taxes due, their wages lost, and their jobs gone forever.

Ninety days later, 424 suits were consolidated against the United States, brought on behalf of 8,485 people living and working in and around Texas City. In other words, the survivors.

In October opening arguments began before U.S. Judge Thomas M. Kennerly of the Southern District of the Federal Court of the United States. The seventy-three-year-old judge loved the United States. His reputation was that of an immovable object, a stiff-backed Christian who saw the world without shades of gray.

The Texas City case was a test case for the new tort reform. The entire legal system, as well as other groups of plaintiffs—African Americans wanting reparation for slavery, Native Americans seeking restoration of lands, soldiers accusing their generals of negligence in sending them into battle— all were hanging on what Kennerly would rule.

The question was simple: Is the government responsible for what happened in Texas City?

The lawyers for the plaintiffs showed by good and sufficient reason that their clients had been victims of a terrible tragedy. No one denied that. The government's case was to shift blame onto the dead, who could be counted on not to speak for themselves. Some were called to give testimony that they saw sailors smoking. Some were hammered because this was the first and only accident of this kind although fifty thousand tons of ammonium nitrate had been transported through Texas City over the years. The dead were calumniated because they had not taken proper precautions.

The lawyers traced the movement of the peacetime shipments directly to the White House and President Truman's answer to General MacArthur's request.

In the end, to everyone's amazement, Kennerly ruled for the plaintiffs on the basis of the single condemnation: "It will not do to say that Defendant . . . could not reasonably foresee that more than 500 people would be killed.

"Defendant did know."

Of course, the case went to the Circuit Court of Appeals, which reversed Kennerly's judgment on a basis that could never have been imagined.

The United States was engaged in a Cold War against communism. Therefore, the victims—the fire chief, the boilermaker, the sea captain, the longshoremen, the factory workers, the ninth-grade chemistry class—were casualties of war. The enemy was at fault, not the U.S. government.

The United States needed ammonium nitrate to fight a war. The king can do no wrong.

Eventually, by a special act passed in 1956, Congress settled all claims for a total of $16.5 million. Their reasoning was that since the chemicals had originated in U.S. ordnance plants, the government must do the right thing. Lyndon Johnson, Texas's senate majority leader, sponsored and shoehorned the bill through.

To this day the results of ammonium nitrate are everywhere. The twenty-first century need only look where the Murrah Building in Oklahoma City stood, destroyed by a disappointed ex-soldier who rented a truck, bought some fertilizer, soaked it with fuel oil, threw in a match, and ran like hell.

As for Fritz Haber, the German scientist and Nobel Prize winner for chemistry who devised ammonium nitrate as a solution to Malthus's theory: In September 1921, forty-five hundred tons of ammonium nitrate blew up in the huge plant in Oppau. As many as a thousand citizens died. And the city was destroyed.

It was Fritz Haber's plant.

"Oh Where, Oh Where"

(Sung to the tune of "The River Is Wide," whose roots go back to
England's "O Wailie, Wailie")

Oh where, oh where is my sweet child?
Oh where, oh where, my heart, is she?
A blinding light, a flash of fire,
And she was gone away from me.

They told me such a thing was naught,
Though sky be dark, though air be foul.
The light of day has gone fore'er.
My heart will ne'er be whole again.

And they who should have treasured all
Were those whose words we should not trust.
My heart, she's gone. Her life is spent.
And all her bright dreams turned to dust.

A thousand mothers weep with me.
A thousand children they have lost.
Too weary they to seek the ones
Whose acts their lives have paid the cost.

Oh where, oh where is my sweet child?
Oh where, oh where, my heart, is she?
A blinding light, a flash of fire,
And she was gone fore'er from me.

8

A HIDEOUS DARKNESS

One minute the sun is bright, the air is still; the next, an impenetrable darkness like midnight. Howling wind. Merciless sheets of pelting rain. Hailstones to draw blood from any exposed skin or to knock a man unconscious if one struck his head.

People in Texas know all these signs. The trouble is, the signs sweep over the horizon into their midst before they can take shelter.

Nevertheless, as they went about their business in Waco, Texas, on that steamy May 11, 1953, they glanced ever over their shoulders to the southwest, knowing that tornadoes most often dip down there to rampage northeast. As the horizon darkened and became more ominous, knowledgeable people realized they were in for more than a welcome rainfall needed by the farmers.

The Amicable Building was the headquarters of the Amicable Life Insurance Company as well as of the First National Bank. To symbolize the strength and solidarity of his business, Artemas Roberts, the company's owner, had built the tallest building in Waco. He guaranteed it would withstand anything, including a tornado. Completed in 1911, it had 3.72 million pounds of steel and 230,000 pounds of iron. It had its own generator and a steam-heating plant to assure its warmth in winter.

It did not have air conditioning. As the storm clouds approached, employees were dispatched to close the windows. People today can only imagine what a job that must have been. The building's 405 rooms on twenty-two floors had 733 windows. Fortunately, they rode up in elevators.

Ira Baden from Dallas had been in the Amicable basement for several hours. He was employed by Nichols Engineering to install four sets of auto-

Advertising poster for a presentation at the library twenty-eight years after the tornado. Courtesy the Waco-McLennan County Library.

matic doors. One set hadn't fit properly, so he was trimming the doors down with a power sizer.

He should have been finished and on his way back to Dallas, but he and his coworker had arrived late. They had driven fast from Hillsboro, thirty-three miles north. Indeed, they had driven quite a bit faster than they intended to. The speedometer would hold steady at seventy-five, then suddenly spin upward. Once it indicated their speed was ninety-five and then one hundred miles per hour.

Baden was alarmed. "We're hitting air pockets," he observed. "This thing keeps trying to run away from us."

Both men knew they were coming into an area of low pressure where a bad storm might be likely to come in at any minute. When they arrived at the Amicable Building at 2:15 P.M., they set to work immediately.

At four o'clock, just as the rain began to fall, Baden went upstairs to the ground-level entrance. People coming in for the shift change commented on the darkness and the blowing wind, but no one seemed particularly worried.

An old Huaco Indian legend proclaimed the land on the banks of the Brazos, where a clear spring gushed forth, to be immune to the mighty winds and storms that struck the countryside around them. Waco was built in a favorable place. It would never be struck by tornadoes.

Across Austin Avenue, dwarfed by the Amicable, stood the R. T. Dennis Building, only five stories high. It was also a town institution. Its switchboard operator, Miss Lillie Matkin, had been on the job for thirty-three years. On down the main street of the town of seventy-five thousand people were the Joy Movie Theatre, a dress shop, City Hall, and a drugstore, as well as other small shops. It was an American main street before shopping malls turned those areas into ghost towns.

At four o'clock that Monday afternoon, the double feature was almost over at the Joy. Robert Mitchum and Susan Hayward were finally getting to a passionate resolution of their Western conflicts in *The Lusty Men*.

Elsewhere, people were thinking about closing up to start home for the evening. A few minutes in their cars or on the bus, which most working people rode, and they'd be home ready to visit with their families before the evening meal.

When the sky opened up with such a heavy shower, most people probably shook their heads in disgust. If the rain had only held off another hour. . . .

The oppressive clouds moved steadily northward. Their bottoms looked like pendulous black bags. No one had ever seen anything like them. As they moved closer, the wind increased until, Baden observed, it sounded like a "power saw in a wet board." A shower turned into a downpour.

At 4:30 P.M., thunder rumbled so loudly that people in the Joy Theatre heard it and felt its vibration. At Walgreen's Drugstore, the store barometer registered 29.2.

People already heading homeward began to hurry. A mighty big storm was headed their way.

Baden had hung the last door and gone into the Walgreen's Pharmacy inside the Amicable Building for a cup of coffee. The rain was falling. Wind was blowing in gusts strong enough to knock a man down. Baden's ears popped. "I felt light-headed," he remembered.

At 4:35 the wind dropped completely. It was deadly calm and growing dark.

Baden came out of the pharmacy and glanced at his newly installed doors, guaranteed to be wind resistant. One was ajar, inching toward the street. He realized that low pressure must be sucking it outward. Quickly, he opened it all the way and propped it in place.

All true Texans are weather watchers. Baden's curiosity got the better of him. He stepped out onto the sidewalk, keeping a hold on the steel rail set into the concrete to guide pedestrian traffic to the proper side of the automatic doors. No sooner was he outside the portico than the wind hit him broadside. He grasped the rail and crouched. A steel mailbox hurtled past, only inches from his head. Clamping one arm around the steel rail, he saw what happened next—from the inside looking up.

Two months later he sold his story to *The Saturday Evening Post*.

The hail began to fall. Not just marble-sized, but hen-egg-sized pellets dented the cars and cracked their windshields. Canvas awnings over the sidewalks intended to shade and protect passersby split and shredded.

The tornado, on the outskirts of town at that moment, skipped over Baylor Stadium. At first the funnel appeared narrow, but then it widened until Al Blackwell, a motorcycle patrolman looking at it from eight miles away, estimated that it was between a half a mile and a mile wide.

The minute it touched down, some people ran for their cars and headed north. Those parked or already driving south had their hoods popped up and blown backwards. The heavy pieces of metal turned into missiles capable of dealing death and destruction at two hundred plus miles an hour. The hail smashed huge dents in the tops of the cars. The wind blew heavy vehicles down the street no matter how hard the owners stomped on the brakes. Those that tried to turn east or west or pulled out of the lee of buildings to cross intersections were blown side-top-side-wheels. With drivers inside they tumbled down the street until they crashed into buildings that were themselves crumbling.

Many cars that did not roll freakishly away were buried under piles of rubble by the buildings falling on them. Some people were crushed in their cars or suffocated in them because they could not be reached in time.

The air was full of pieces of roofs, lumber, and shards of glass all whirling in slow motion up into the clouds. Some people thought they saw bodies flying through the air and crashing into the street in front of them. A closer look helped them recognize the forms as mannequins sucked out of store windows.

People who sought to go to the aid of others hesitated when telephone poles standing along the streets went down "like pins in a bowling alley."

One man's car started rolling backwards down the street. He jumped out, but the wind knocked him over. He crawled on his belly until he reached a plum tree. He wrapped his arms around the low trunk and held on as he was literally stretched out in the air and whipped back and forth like a rag. His clothes were ripped from his body, and his face was covered with mud.

At the Cotton Palace Park, Billy Betros, the son of the chief of police, and three other boys had gone for a swim after school. The boys, the lifeguards, and the pool manager took shelter in the basement.

The barometer in the drugstore fell to the bottom. The extreme low pressure was popping more than ears. Doors swung open. Windows shattered outward, and the glass blew away on the wind as the pressure in the buildings equalized with that outside. Light bulbs began to pop. But no one really cared. The electricity had gone out all over town.

Amazingly, the Amicable Building that Artemas Roberts had built to stand against hurricanes swayed but did not crumble. People even on the top floor looked at each other in alarm and perhaps grabbed the edges of their desks, but the building did not fall.

On the steps of the Amicable, Ira Baden still clung for dear life to the steel-pipe railing. Although he could not see the wind, he knew he was in the middle of a tornado. Flying debris heading straight for his face would suddenly curve away and swirl upward. In helpless horror, he watched as the top four floors of the five-story Dennis Building were wrenched upward. Above the remaining first floor, they exploded in the air, then collapsed back at an angle in a gigantic pile of rubble that partially collapsed the roof of the Joy Theatre and the Torrance Recreation Hall.

The patrons in the Dennis, the store owners Ed and Rush Berry, and twenty-three employees, including the switchboard operator, were buried.

Inside the movie theatre, the screen went black as all the lights went out. The outside wall of the building began to tumble outward as the roof on the side next to the Dennis Building crashed in.

The audience, comprising mostly small children and their mothers, began to scream and stampede up the aisle. As they burst into the lobby, the sights through the thick glass doors froze them in their tracks. Some must have thought they had run into another movie.

Buildings were crumbling in front of them. Debris tumbled into the street, landing on their parked cars. The air was full of flying, whirling objects—bricks, shards of glass, pieces of metal, and strips of wood.

On the floors above the ground, the chaos was unimaginable. People on these upper floors scrambled under their desks as the ceilings crashed down. Then, they too were crushed as the floor dropped beneath them, sending them falling onto the floors beneath, sometimes on people like themselves trying to take shelter.

Screams of terror and pain stopped abruptly or were drowned in the roar of the wind and the rumble of debris.

At 4:35 P.M., Gloria Mae Dobrovolney, her father, and Barbara Johnson had driven downtown to buy parakeet seed. Gloria let her father off to go inside the Texas Seed Company. She and her friend began to circle the block.

A naval veteran, Sam Edwards, heard a sound like a destroyer salvo. For two minutes the rain and hail poured from the skies in a blinding, deadly torrent. Then came a lull like a movie cliché.

It was "quiet. Too quiet."

Sam felt as if his eardrums were going to burst. He heard a girl's scream. He turned to see the top of the building across the street "heave up and down like a canvas top."

Gloria's father stood in the entrance of the Texas Seed Company. He was motioning for the girls to come in. Barbara jumped out and dashed for the entrance. As her friend ran into the building, Gloria slid from under the wheel across the seat toward the door. Before she could get clear of the car, the Texas Seed Company collapsed. The roof of her car with her inside was crushed by the falling bricks.

Minutes later, when people were able to free her from her car, she ran to the wreck of the building and began digging frantically. The rain was falling so hard, they could not see the tears coursing down her cheeks.

"I saw Dad standing there by the door, waving for me to come in where I'd be safe, and then there were only falling bricks and mortar. Dad was under it all."

At 4:37 P.M., the state highway patrol received a report of wind damage on the southeast side of town. Three minutes later, while the monster was doing its damnedest to destroy the entire town, the first telephone call came in for an ambulance. In all likelihood the call came from the trunk line run out of the Amicable Building, which was swaying but standing in the middle of the devastation.

Then, the worst was over.

The tornado hopscotched the last few blocks north, jumped the Brazos, and roared on out of the city. It took the roof off the empty East Waco Elementary School and the brick front off the Turner Street Baptist Church. Ten minutes later, it roared away, heading northeast out of town. True to the usual behavior of its kind, it bounded along through McLennan County for twenty-three miles before it rained itself out within sight of the little community of Axtell.

Like a bomb going off in a surprise attack, it had wreaked incredible damage and caused numerous deaths and many, many injuries.

In the buildings still standing on Austin Street, all of the able-bodied stumbled out into the street in the pouring rain to begin rescue efforts. One man staggered down the street from what was left of the Torrance recreation area. "It's a miracle—a miracle," he stammered. "Everybody dead there but me—a miracle."

The clock stopped at 4:40 P.M. on the marquee of the First National Bank headquartered in the Amicable Building.

No amount of preparation could have made any difference.

Notorious Tornado Alley is a ten-state area stretching north from Texas to include Oklahoma, Arkansas, Kansas, Nebraska, Missouri, Iowa, Illinois, Indiana, and Colorado. Tornadoes occur most frequently there. People living elsewhere have no reason to believe themselves entirely safe. All fifty states, including Alaska and Hawaii, have experienced tornadoes. Some of the most violent storms with the largest loss of life have occurred in Alabama, Mississippi, Michigan, and Massachusetts. Florida has a large number of twisters, but they are generally less devastating than those on the dry plains.

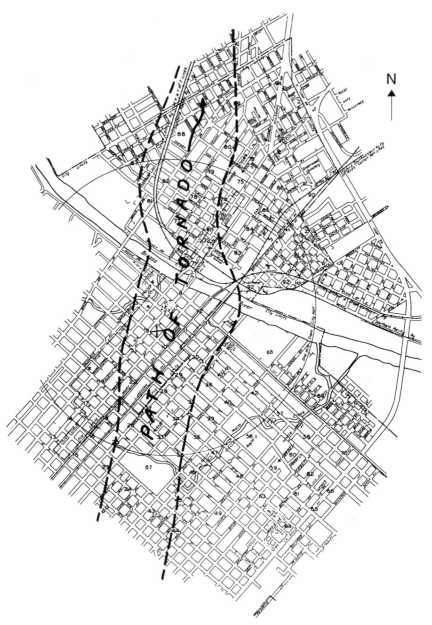

N

The path of the tornado. Courtesy the Waco-McLennan County Library.

Tornadoes are violently rotating columns of air that come in contact with the ground. They descend from a thunderstorm that has begun to move counterclockwise around a low-pressure area. Hurricanes have the same motion.

Three conditions are required for the thunderstorms to form. The first is warm, humid air. Late spring is the most dangerous time, when the ground warms in the sun and the stored winter moisture begins to evaporate. At this time of year, the days are balmy, the birds are singing, new life is awakening. People are generally unaware that anything may be about to occur. Even if they were aware, there would be little they could do. Tornadoes and their big uncles, the hurricanes, are unbelievably destructive.

Warm air rises rapidly into the upper atmosphere, where the weather becomes more unstable. Once aloft, the air cools and condenses into towering cumulus clouds, famously called thunderheads. The word "cumulus" comes from the Latin word meaning to "heap." The cumulus clouds begin to accumulate and pile themselves higher and higher. As they pile, they gather more and more moisture and compress it. Observers are then actually seeing the second condition necessary for the formation of tornadoes.

The third condition is the logical extension of the other two. The heated air becomes a lifting force. As hot air rises, masses of cool air rush in on the ground to take its place. A circular vertical motion begins. The cool breezes turn into high winds that push more hot moist air up where it packs the clouds.

The next visible result is mammatocumulus clouds. They look like black bags hanging from the bottoms of the thunderheads. By that time the air has climbed so high in the thunderheads that at the top of the updraft the moisture freezes and turns to hailstones—from the size of peas or marbles to the size of softballs. In the midst of these destructive thunderstorms, tornadoes are born. The whole mass begins to whirl horizontally at greater and greater speed like a giant screw around a pressure area that falls steadily lower.

The anatomy of a tornado has been studied and divided into four stages, thanks to intrepid storm chasers such as those glamorized in Michael Crichton's movie *Twister*.

The first stage appears ahead of the storm. Increased wind turns to gusts when the rain falls into hot, dry air. At that point, a rotating, vertical motion starts, and the supercell is formed. At this point the National Weather Service may send out a tornado watch message, alerting people to the possibility of tornadoes.

Hurricanes at sea often form waterspouts within their supercell. These are visible to the naked eye, but tornadoes in the air above land are invisible.

Heavy rain and hail fall from the supercell, or core. Within that downpour tornadoes have already formed, but often have not touched down. Storm chasers try to find these tornadoes generated in the second stage of the storm. They try to "punch the core" by actually driving into the moving supercell. Obviously, they are headed into a potentially deadly place in search of a tornado to chase.

The third stage excites the storm chasers because they can actually see it on weather radar. It's the tornado's signature, the hook. The rain and hail wrap around the circling air. It looks like a hook emerging from the core. When the National Weather Service sees these "hook echoes," it sends out tornado warnings. These undoubtedly save many lives. But when a tornado drops down in a crowded business district or a thickly populated suburb, no amount of warning can prevent the destruction and loss of life.

The fourth stage comes when people think the storm is over. The "rear flank downdrafts" form when the tornado moves through dry air, which is sucked up into the middle of the storm. It causes the rain and hail to evaporate. Their drafts then plunge out of the storm to do more damage as they form again.

A tornado's aftermath is usually as bad as or worse than the actual moments of a disaster, if for no other reason than that the one is over in minutes while the other may last a decade. The damage left behind was reminiscent of Berlin in 1945. Two square miles of the city were ruined. On Austin Avenue only three buildings had been spared: the Roosevelt Hotel, the City Hall, and the Amicable Building. All of those had suffered wind and water damage.

Survivors in standing buildings a few blocks from Austin and Franklin avenues poured out into the streets to help their friends. What they found in the ruins was the stuff of horror movies. Dashing into the scene, in many cases they were in imminent danger of being killed or injured. Live power lines snaked through the rubble. A pool of water might deliver a shock severe enough to stop a man's heart. Gas from broken mains seeped through the wreckage, but the drenching rain probably lessened the danger of fire.

Many survivors could see little but destroyed buildings and piles of rubble. Many must have thought of the hopelessness of the situation. How could anyone be alive under all of that?

Surprisingly few people rushed to the scene from outside the area. Citizens in other parts of town discounted the stories they heard coming over the radio station because when they stepped out into their yards, they saw the towering Amicable Building and assumed the reports were exaggerated. A bus driver driving his route had no real concept of what had happened until he was in the center of it. Whether out of shock or disbelief, he carefully detoured around the debris and actually picked up mothers and children from the Joy Theatre before proceeding on his way.

On Austin Avenue, many survivors were too dazed to take in what had happened to them. They were observed doing irrational things. One man whose clothes had been ripped from his body walked down the street stark naked, his expression unconcerned.

When a waitress was asked to keep another man's coat so he could go outside to help the injured, she carefully folded it and placed it in the refrigerator.

Every ambulance in the city turned on its siren and rushed downtown. The gas company shut off the mains, the Red Cross gathered its staff plus all its usual volunteers, and the Texas Power and Light loaded up two auxiliary generators and transported them into the area.

All this happened within minutes, when most people in Waco did not know that anything had happened at all. The speed with which the storm vanished fooled everyone not directly in its path. Tommy Turner, central Texas correspondent for the *Dallas Morning News,* received a call from his editor in Dallas.

"What happened in Waco?"

Turner was taken aback. "What do you mean?"

"We hear you've had a tornado."

Turner replied that they'd had some hail and high winds.

"Well, maybe you'd better check on the rumor."

Within hours Mayor Ralph Wolf abandoned City Hall, and city officials moved into the Amicable, which had its own generators. Major General G. P. Disosway, in charge of flight training at James Connally Air Force Base, sent in his men and equipment. At the same time, he urged Wolf to keep command of the rescue operation.

Taking the general's advice, Mayor Wolf set up command central in the Amicable Building across the street from the Dennis Building, which had disintegrated into a pile of rubble fifteen feet high. All along the street, airmen, working under floodlights also from the base, were digging into the piles of rubble.

Under one pile was Lillie Matkin, the switchboard operator, who had remained at her post. Not until 6:30 P.M., two hours after the disaster, did anyone hear her cries for help. Efforts to reach her stalled almost immediately. How could her rescuers reach her without killing her?

By this time ambulance sirens howled almost continuously up and down the street as bodies both living and dead were uncovered and rushed away. Survivors pointed out piles of rubble that covered people. In one case Ira Baden came across a man's bare feet sticking out from under a pile of bricks. He felt for the pulse in the ankle, shook his head, and moved on.

By now the darkness was the darkness of night. Police cordoned off the devastated sections and held back a crowd that had grown to thousands. Many had come to volunteer but were not needed because of the organized effort in the relatively small area. Many were praying for lost friends and family. Many had simply come to gape.

Before five o'clock, Lieutenant Colonel Wiley Stem of the Texas National Guard had reported to Mayor Wolf. Unfortunately, he could not order the guard to snap into action because communications were down all over the city. Moreover, the guard had its own problems. The tornado had struck the armory, damaging it badly. The roof had peeled back, all the windows were blown out, and heavy rains poured in. Men were trapped in the debris.

Not until six o'clock did someone find an emergency telephone to place a call to Austin. At 6:30 Governor Allen Shivers was notified. He called Fourth Army Headquarters at San Antonio and ordered the army to head for the beleaguered city. An abbreviated group of thirty-six men and officers reached Waco at 10:00 that evening. The failure to make an instant response impressed upon the governor the need to create a disaster plan to be in place for the next time.

Not until three hours after the strike was the National Guard ordered to move officially. By that time 90 percent of the officers and men in the Waco units had reported voluntarily to the downtown area.

By 11:00 P.M., Miss Lillie Matkin had been entombed over six hours. Rescuers had drilled a hole down to her, but a new problem surfaced. Gas fumes from broken pipes had begun to slip through the wreckage. She begged for some oxygen, complaining that she couldn't breathe. Another time she asked for ice to hold in her mouth.

The young men who sat with her through the long ordeal were Sergeant J. D. Smith of Bossier City, Louisiana, and Airman Second Class Dennis Scholtz of Detroit, Michigan. They took turns talking to her and giving her ice, oxygen, and coffee.

Freeing her was a more serious problem than anyone realized at first. Pulling the debris off her was almost impossible for fear of dislodging a major piece and crushing her beneath a released weight. Tunneling underneath was likewise impossible. She was under two floors of the building that kept subsiding slowly into the basement.

Throughout the night they could hear the crack of porcelain appliances, part of the store's merchandise. Supports around her were slowly disintegrating under the pressure. With every sound the problem became more acute.

Meanwhile, the search for missing persons continued, although now the searchers were sure that everyone they found would be dead. At 1:00 A.M. they uncovered W. J. Dobrovolney's body. His daughter, Gloria Mae, had seen the Texas Seed Company building fall on him. Four hours later they found the body of her friend, Barbara Johnson. Because Gloria had had to scramble across the seat of the car and had not made it into the building, she had lived.

The Torrance Recreation Hall had seventeen bodies in it, including that of a promising high school athlete, six-foot-four, 260-pound Kay Sharbutt. He had been crushed under a pile of debris. His watch had stopped at 4:45.

Now the faces of the onlookers were white, and many turned away as hopes and prayers were dashed.

At last at 6:55 A.M., Miss Lillie Matkin was freed. She had been lying on her side with her knees drawn up almost to her chest for over fourteen hours. As she was carried to the ambulance, she asked her rescuers to please get her shoes. Her next request was for a steak dinner—right away.

Someone put her shoes in the ambulance, and she was taken to Providence Hospital. The doctors discovered she had a black eye, a cut arm, and deep bruises on her chest, her hip, and her leg. Mostly she suffered from shock.

Her ordeal was described by reporter Woody Barron, who had crawled through a tunnel in the debris and described the tunnel from below.

"We could smell gas escaping from the broken mains. Water was running in torrents from broken pipes in the building. We could hear it gurgling through the piles of junk. [We] . . . could hear hundreds of rescue workers on top of the debris, trying to dig their way through to victims."

Police Sergeant Eddie Betros spent the evening and night keeping traffic moving and sending the curious on their way from the downtown. Occasionally, someone would ask him about his son who had been swimming. Betros would merely nod quietly. When rescuers found the four boys, who had taken shelter in the basement at the Cotton Palace Park, all four had been crushed beneath the crumbling wall.

On May 12 the city declared Ambulance Day. The vehicles had been in constant use since 4:40 P.M., May 11. Private cars displaying white cloths on their radio antennas had supplemented them. The two main hospitals were packed to overflowing, as were the infirmary at James Connally Air Force Base and the Veterans Administration facilities.

The medical ward clerks had given up trying to take information. When identification was possible, they wrote the information, usually just the name and address, on tape and stuck it on the person's forehead. At least once they stuck it on a person who was either dead on arrival or dead within minutes before any medical treatment could get to him.

With all the rooms and wards filled, the staff lined the injured along corridors and in waiting rooms. Their moans and pleas added to the confusion and sense of helplessness felt by health care workers who had never in their lives confronted anything of this magnitude.

Back on Austin Avenue, a crane operator lifted a section of wall from the Dennis Building. Embedded in it were the bodies of two women. Men cursed and wept at the sight as workers covered the bodies with blankets.

In the end fifty-six bodies were recovered from the block between Austin and Franklin avenues and Fourth and Fifth streets. Thirty-eight were recovered in the square around City Hall.

In all, 114 persons were killed or fatally injured in the space of ten minutes; 1,097 sustained injuries that required treatment from a physician. It was the tenth deadliest tornado in American history to date.

Two thousand automobiles were demolished or severely damaged and eight hundred fifty homes throughout the twenty-three-mile area were destroyed or partially wrecked. The business district suffered the losses of 196 buildings completely demolished; 376 buildings were declared unsafe to return to. Eventually 396 buildings were torn down.

Property damage was estimated at $51 million—a huge bill in 1953, when a good salary for an ordinary working person was $2,500 to $3,000 a year.

More significant was the psychological damage to the heart of the town. In effect, it killed it. People no longer went into the downtown district, whether from bad memories or uneasiness. A big suburban shopping center appeared, and merchants put their new businesses in there rather than back into downtown. As in Galveston, which lost so much of its beach and

Children playing in the "surprise" fountain on Fair Day downtown. Author photo.

its industrial district, the town's growth was slowed. While the island city rebuilt itself literally from the ground up, Waco did very little. It seemed to have lost its vitality. While the rest of Texas's urban areas began to increase in size, Waco stayed approximately the same. In so doing it lost the race to become a major city.

Racial problems of the 1960s contributed to "white flight" from the town itself. The population declined, and Connally Air Force Base closed in 1966.

The city now has a population of 110,000. It has not grown the way other urban centers in Texas have. Twenty-five years passed before an urban renewal project of $125 million in 1978 resulted in the town's creating a small museum complex to include the Texas Ranger Hall of Fame and Museum and the Texas Sports Hall of Fame. The *Brazos Queen* riverboat was purchased to take advantage of the waterfront. A convention and shopping center opened near Baylor University with its world famous Browning Library.

Still, one may say that the tornado marked a turning point for the city. The Amicable Building became the Amaco Building. It still stands looming over the paved area called Heritage Square, where the town holds craft fairs, county activities, and concerts. The fountain in the center is a strange fountain. Really no fountain at all, it is a series of holes in the flat pavement. Water spouts up from these holes at random intervals. Otherwise, nothing is seen above ground.

Did the people who commissioned it fear that building a more traditional fountain with basin and structure above ground would tempt the gods of the winds and the darkness?

The rain, hail, and darkness in the bright spring afternoon cut a swath two miles long and a mile wide through downtown Waco. The destruction it wrought has lasted for half a century. The Huaco's myth was dispelled, and a pleasant city's peace was destroyed for years.

Where other Texas cities have grown huge and prospered, Waco has remained about the same, a university town without any particular interest in growing bigger and giving its own youth reasons to stay there and grow with it. Perhaps the entrepreneurial spirit was sucked up into the heart of black mammatocumulus clouds and whirled away in the hideous darkness.

"And Give Him Shelter from the Storm"
(A love song played on a guitar)

A man has only hands and heart
To keep his family safe from harm.
He's overmatched when darkness falls,
And there's no shelter from the storm.

For nature's power, the mighty wind
Can sweep away all he would save.
The towers of stone, the rotten iron
Become the clods that make his grave.

A woman's love is precious gold.
Her touch alone will keep him warm.
She is the shield around his heart
To give him shelter from the storm.

Her words can call him from the brink.
Her touch upon his brow can heal.
If she'll but speak his name aloud,
He'll heed her words and break death's seal.

Through darkness dire their hands reach forth,
Their clasp, a link in mortal form.
From 'neath the stone, she'll call him back
And give him shelter from the storm.

9

THE RICHEST LITTLE SCHOOL
DISTRICT IN THE WORLD

About six miles southeast of London, Texas, deep in the Piney Woods, a pair of crazy old coots reckoned to drill for oil and gas. The year was 1929, the cotton crop had failed, and East Texas was in the depths of a depression that would engulf the entire United States in a very few months. "Dad" Joiner and "Doc" Lloyd were wildcatters who leased a 975-acre tract in the woods. They erected a derrick made of scrap lumber and dilapidated machinery, named it Daisy Bradford No. 1 in honor of the lessee, and sank a well that had to be abandoned when the drill jammed in the hole at 1,095 feet.

Joiner, the promoter of the pair, sold $25-share certificates to people around Rusk County to finance another try. The crew moved the rig west a hundred feet, named it Daisy Bradford No. 2, and drilled again. At two thousand feet the pipe hung in the hole, and the second well had to be abandoned.

Again Dad sold $25 certificates to waitresses, postal clerks, policemen, and railroad workers. Again the crew moved the well, now Daisy Bradford No. 3, a hundred feet to the west, and again they began to drill. By that time practically everyone in Rusk County had a piece of that forlorn enterprise. It became their hope. William Tucker, the banker from Overton a mile away, frequently left work and drove over to the Daisy Bradford No. 3 to help out until dark. His wife cooked dinner for the crew.

At 3,536 feet Ed Laster, the driller, pulled up a core sample that had nine inches of oil-saturated sand at the bottom. Knowledgeable oilmen discounted the sample. They believed Laster had "salted the well" to procure more investment. But rumors spread. Excitement grew. People began to trade leases. Dad was able to borrow more money.

On October 1, eighteen days before Black Monday, when the New York stock market crashed five hundred points, people began gathering at the well. The crowd swelled to eight thousand people. They were tired and uncomfortable, but nobody left.

Late in the afternoon of October 3, a gurgling noise came from the pipe. Laster yelled to the crew to douse the fire. As he did, a stream of oil bubbled up out of the hole. People watched with open mouths as it gained volume and height. It rose past the pipes, past the monkey board that encircled the top of the derrick, past the cobbled up wreck of the rig into the sunset-streaked Texas sky.

Oil and gas for everyone to see from their last, best hope—Daisy Bradford No. 3. No one at that moment knew that East Texas, a four-hundred-square-mile oil field, had blown in. In its seventy-five-year history, over thirty-two thousand wells were drilled. Fewer than five hundred were dry holes. To this day forty-four hundred wells produce forty-five thousand barrels a day.

Everybody owned a little piece of the action, including most of the citizens in the little town of London with a hundred homes, a handful of stores, and a school population of one hundred in ten grades of study.

North of London, Humble Oil and Refining, former governor Ross Sterling's company, purchased a tract of land and set up a headquarters and company camp. One hundred families relocated from his fields in Corsicana, and the town of New London was born.

On the other end of the tract, H. L. Hunt, a gambler from Arkansas who had purchased some of Dad Joiner's leases, set up his Parade Company. Eventually, H. L. Hunt bought Joiner out and began to accumulate the incredible wealth that earned him the reputation of the richest man in America.

The population of the town soon grew to one thousand, all young people with young families. The first grade alone had eighty-five students. Two ward schools had to be built to accommodate the growing school population. Together they formed the London Independent School District, which had an unbelievable assessed value of $16 million.

Money ran like oil upon the ground, and the people could afford the very best for their children. In 1932 on the site of the ward schools, they erected a $350,000 school complex with beautiful hardwood floors in every classroom. The students learned in laboratories for science, business, and manual training. They presented plays in an auditorium with a fully equipped stage and balcony. Every room was equipped with gas radiators to keep the students warm. Announcements and weekly Christian devotionals were delivered over a schoolwide intercom system, just like in the big schools in Dallas and Houston.

Such wealth as oil and gas provided had never been imagined, let alone seen. Such a school would have been beyond the wildest dreams of the farmers and ranchers before they suddenly became millionaires.

The East Texas oil field continued to grow as more and more producing wells were drilled. The need for a larger school became apparent. A new brick elementary building, built north of the high school, was already too small when it was completed. In 1936–1937 the fifth graders were moved from the bursting elementary building into the junior high school wing. A wooden gymnasium and a football field with bleachers were added. More classrooms were added in the form of two-story wings, shaping the building like a large letter "E" with thirty thousand square feet of floor space.

The wealth was such that someone merely had to suggest that the school might need some new facility, and it was bought or built or both. Such wealth flowed from the ground in a seemingly endless stream. Three other separate facilities were deemed necessary, including a home-economics cottage, a frame music building, and a brick cafeteria. The first outdoor stadium lights in East Texas were added to the football field.

Somewhere in the neighborhood of twelve hundred students were now enrolled, enjoying opportunities unheard of in the rest of Texas. Students read the latest books purchased unstintingly by the librarians. The Wildcat Marching Band toured the state in a trailer bus and played new compositions by notable musicians in special concerts.

Scheduled for Friday, March 19, 1937, was a day-long Inter-Scholastic League competition some twelve miles away in Henderson. Superintendent C. W. Shaw had canceled school for that day. All the students not directly involved in the contests were encouraged to travel there to show support for the writing, mathematics, speech, and business competitions, as well as the track and baseball events. Hopes were high for New London to lead the district.

Like a dream of a perfect American town, the school was the center of the community. All the students attended unless they were sick. In all that large student body, only about two dozen were absent on Thursday, March

18, 1937. Of that number only four boys were discovered playing hooky at a movie theatre in Arp.

Tradition had been broken that day in two ways. First, the principal had asked upper-grade students to remain at school for extra training for the Inter-Scholastic League competition the following day. Second, the PTA would ordinarily have met in the auditorium. Instead, they met in the gym at 3:00 to watch the students from the fifth grade perform Mexican dances for their entertainment.

When the program was over at about 3:15, the teacher told the dancers to leave the building and get on the waiting buses rather than go back to the classrooms for fifteen minutes more.

At 3:17, Mr. L. R. Butler, the teacher of the manual-training class, decided to test a student's repair job on his project. With some of his fifteen students standing at his side and the others around the room working on other things, he plugged in a belt sander.

A spark jumped, and in the words of surviving student John Dial, who had been standing next to the machine, "It was like being in the middle of a flash of lightning." John Nelson, who was standing farther away, remembered "a big mess of sand and what looked like a ball of fire tumbled into the room. Something hit me in the leg. It knocked me down, but I scrambled up and rushed outside."

At the moment of ignition, a fireball ripped into the occupied workshop, fed by the odorless, tasteless, and colorless natural gas that had leaked from the poorly ventilated space beneath the floor into the classroom to mix unnoticed with the air. From that initial spark, the fire burst outward in all directions.

Ralph Carr, a Tidewater Oil Company employee, was sitting in his office across the street from the school. He looked out his window and thought his eyes were fooling him. "The school was just raised up and hung in the air." After a split second, it fell, with the walls caving and crumbling to fill the vacuum created by the force of the explosion. Bricks from the walls, chunks of concrete from the foundation, steel framework, red roof tiles, hardwood flooring, and school desks fell inward, crashing down, smashing, flattening more rooms that had not been blown away but now were underneath the rain of debris. And into the melee fell the bodies of hundreds of children.

Little Mollie Sealy was a fifth-grader who had danced the Mexican hat dance. Sitting on board the bus quietly waiting, she saw the school go up. "It was just a gray cloud that went up and up and up. I just never thought it was going to come down. Then the building collapsed. Big chunks of concrete went flying, some across the highway."

Another student, Peggy Harris, never heard a noise. "It was silent. Just a huge vacuum. No noise at all." Indeed, many students never remembered hearing the blast, probably because the concussion of it had deafened and momentarily knocked them unconscious.

John Nelson, who had run outside after the explosion in the shop, had a "funny sort of feeling" that forced him to sit down on the ground. Then, he looked up and saw his own sister hanging unconscious on a window pane. Galvanized by fear for her, he scaled the wall that had become a pile of rubble to rescue her. With her safe, he ran back into the building and dragged out a friend with a broken ankle. When he went back inside a third time, he found five of his friends and Mr. Butler dead.

Children on the second floor of the doomed, crumbling building were not spared any of the horror or terror. Some were killed instantly by chunks of concrete hurtling through the floors. Those who could began to jump for their lives. An elementary school teacher, Mrs. Tom Parmley, was supervising children on the playground. She started immediately gathering hurt children into nearby cars. As she helped, dragged, carried them to the relative safety, she was almost hit several times by children jumping from the upper-story windows.

More bricks, chunks of wood, shards of blackboard slate, and blocks of concrete turned into deadly missiles that plowed through the thin interior walls of the classrooms, killing people where they sat at their desks. Mattie Queen Price, the private music tutor, was killed instantly sitting at her desk in her office. When her brother found her body at the American Legion Hall in Overton, "there was only a small cut on her face, but the back of her head was flat as a pancake and one leg was nearly cut off."

Some students were blown out of the buildings through the upstairs windows, landing on the grounds and in the street. Helen and Marie Beard were leaving the building hand in hand when the explosion occurred. Helen was thrown into the air, hit in the head by a brick, and slammed into an automobile forty feet away. Marie was knocked unconscious and crushed under falling debris. Miraculously, both girls survived.

Superintendent W. C. Shaw was outside the building. Stunned and bleeding from a head wound from flying debris, he quickly became distraught, repeating, "Oh, my God. Those poor children." F. F. Waggoner, the principal, was headed for his office in the building when he paused to

A montage of mistakes. Papers from all over the state printed death tolls as the rumors mounted. Author photo courtesy London Museum.

help a crying child. The explosion crushed the two students studying at his desk in his office.

All sixty-five students in one study hall were killed instantly. In the other study hall, the teacher yelled for her students to get under their desks and ducked under her own. She was trapped immobile for so long that she could not move when she was rescued.

At 3:20 P.M. the first call went in to the Central Telephone operator in Overton, whose banker, William Tucker, had bought into the Daisy Bradford No. 3.

At the same time, the New London band director, C. R. Sory, ran to his car, loaded as many wounded students as he could and drove away. At 3:40 he arrived in Overton and drove first to the Western Union Telegraph Office. He shouted to the operator, "The London School is blown to bits, hundreds killed and injured! Get help!" While the telegraph operator began clicking out the news, Sory drove to the hospital and began unloading his injured children.

A man driving by the school in a bread truck stopped and threw all the bread out onto the ground. He picked up injured students, put them in the

More mistakes mounted on the museum wall beside the telephone switchboard from London that sent out the calls for help. Author photo courtesy London Museum.

truck, and drove off with them to one of the seven small hospitals in the area.

The explosion was heard in the oil fields. At the time of the blast, the school had seven producing wells on its campus. Crews from wells being drilled in the vicinity assumed that a storage tank had blown up, not an uncommon occurrence. By 3:30 they had shut down their rigs and gone to offer aid even before the news flashed, as if by some human telegraph system, that the school had blown sky high. They arrived to find the PTA mothers weeping as they tried to pull the rubble away with their bare hands.

Among the first rescuers was Clyde Sealy, whose daughter Mollie had been waiting on the bus. His wife had been in the gym. The new facility had fortunately been built over dirt, so no gas had accumulated under it. It was spared. As was reasoned later, the auditorium also had dirt beneath its foundation. The rest of the building, constructed with poorly ventilated crawl space beneath the floors, had turned into a huge bomb whose explosion followed the paths of least resistance—inward and upward.

The crews brought with them the heavy equipment, winch trucks and cranes, and acetylene torches. "We worked all night. We attached lines to big slabs of concrete," recalled Sealy. "It was tedious work, because we were afraid we would find a child under" every piece they moved.

As the dust began to settle, a man who was making a delivery of peach baskets stopped. He unloaded the baskets from a factory in Jacksonville, donating them to the rescue efforts, and drove away. His donation proved to be one of the most valuable. For seventeen hours, those baskets were carried deep into the ruins, filled with chunks of concrete, shattered bricks, and unpaired shoes, and passed hand to hand out of the building. Their contents were then gone through piece by piece for human remains before being added to the growing pile of rubble.

At 4:15 President Franklin D. Roosevelt heard of the disaster. He notified the Red Cross, put all the government agencies on standby alert, and telephoned Governor James V. Allred, who had already sent highway patrolmen and Texas Rangers to the scene.

Five minutes later the Salvation Army arrived from Gladewater and began serving sandwiches and coffee. During the twenty-four-hour period, they served thirty-six thousand sandwiches. The American Legionnaires from Overton, Henderson, and Kilgore began to arrive before 5:00.

The largest hospital in the area, Mother Francis in Tyler, had been scheduled to open on the following day. At 5:30 the elaborately planned grand opening was pushed aside. More than a hundred cots were set up, and the entire staff reported for duty within the hour. Surplus medical supplies began to arrive from all over Texas. Drugstores opened their pharmacies and cleared the shelves of bandages, pain relievers, and splints. Anything and everything that might be useful was sent out immediately.

At the same time, the National Guardsmen began to arrive to prevent looting. Pitching in rather than wasting their able bodies standing guard, the men gave their rifles to a troop of First Class Boy Scouts, who stood guard from then on.

As darkness fell, despite everyone's best efforts, the situation was turning chaotic. The ruined building was pitch black inside and choked with dust.

At 6:00 a pair of volunteer electricians climbed to the top of the goal-posts on the football field and attached lights to illuminate the work area. By that time three thousand men were bringing out bodies.

Fifth-grader H. G. White, who had been part of the PTA entertainment, witnessed sights that he could never get out of his head. The men were taking children from the building, carrying them out in their arms and on stretchers. "Some of them had no heads," White recalled, "and the heads of some others rolled off the stretchers when they were carried out."

Despite the lights, inside the ruin was a dark maze filled with fine white dust. The gritty fog was so heavy that it was nearly impossible to see or even to breathe. The children had it imbedded in their skin along with chips of building material, shards of glass, wood splinters, and steel shavings. Possibly some badly injured children suffocated before help could reach them. Likewise, an attending physician theorized that some of the children who were found dead with no apparent injuries died of shock that accompanied the force of the explosion.

Still, deep in the ruins, the survivors, ages eleven through eighteen, wriggled and twisted their bodies, helped each other, coughed and pushed and wept with the absolute surety that outside their parents were waiting for them.

Betty Jo Hardin came to with "everything from bricks to plaster" on her head, pinning her to the desktop. She "wiggled 'til I got my head off my desk and then fell down in the aisle." She remembered—quite philosophically for a seventh-grader—that she just took her time and took one brick off at a time.

Fifteen-year-old Corinne Gary in Miss Thompson's English class found herself completely pinned—head, hands, feet, and body. In her line of vision was a classmate who needed help. Leaving various patches of skin behind, Corinne managed to get loose. In the dark she dropped a ring her father had given her. Determined not to leave anything that she prized behind, she crawled back, felt for the ring, found it, and then crawled to the side of the girl who needed help. When Corinne found she couldn't help her, the girl whispered, "Save yourself and help someone else."

Ike Challis, a fifth-grader, didn't feel any pain until "the rescue workers walked on my head. That's when I started yelling." Later Ike was taken to the Baptist Church in Overton. He reported, "The doctor set me up on a cabinet in the church kitchen and checked me out. I wasn't sent to a hospital, because I only had a fractured skull."

The rescue workers reached a toppled bookcase. The space underneath sheltered ten children. The rescuers heard, "Mister, would you get me out, please?"

"Just a minute, Sonny, we're coming," one of the rescuers called.

"All right," the little boy replied. "I won't make any noise."

He was good as his word, even when they uncovered him to find that his leg was broken.

Further on into the ruins, they discovered no more protected children. Instead, they found twisted and crushed bodies and body parts under chunks of concrete, buried in dust and plaster. In the remains of one room, they found fifty little children tumbled and piled against the remains of a wall. They were every one dead. As the floor had canted upward, they had all been thrown to one side and crushed when the floor was slammed up against the wall. Kilgore fire chief Burk O'Donovan was shaken to the core. "I never saw such a pathetic sight in all my life."

As their children were brought out, the parents rushed forward.

"Is it her?"

"Is it him?"

"Oh, my God. It's him!"

One mother ran back and forth between the bodies of her two boys, who had been blown out of the building. She blew in the mouth of one, saying, "You're not dead! You're not dead!" She hugged him and then ran to the other to do and say the same thing. Finally, some other mothers led her away.

By 8:00 P.M. the area for five miles around the school was placed under martial law. At 8:30 a picket line was set up allowing only ambulances, doctors, nurses, peace officers, rescue workers, newsmen, and relatives through. Since that accounted for almost everyone, the results were less than satisfactory. Some people reported looting, although what could have been looted from the wrecked building and the bodies of the children was questionable.

All over East Texas, oilmen came to help. In particular Haroldson Lafayette Hunt drove over from Dallas. With his "Hunt Men" he helped the devastated fathers lift their children from the wreckage and search for them in the rows of little bodies stretched out on the school grounds and in the hospitals. The Hunt employees worked in pairs to render aid. Hunt himself stuffed hundred dollar bills into the pockets of the grieving men.

The scene outside the wrecked school resembled a combination bombsite and charnel house. Embalmers were already there by the dozens from nearby large cities. The bodies and pieces of bodies of children not yet claimed were lined up. No one will ever be able to discover how many children were actually killed that day.

Some people claimed bodies that were so badly damaged that they actually claimed the wrong child. The parents of Dale May York were especially distraught because their daughter had been absent from school with pneumonia and had returned only that day. They actually buried the child whom they believed to be she, only to find out soon afterward that they had buried Wanda Emberling, whose parents were searching everywhere for her.

At least two bodies were never claimed, probably because the parents misidentified and buried the bodies of other children. Quite a few bodies and pieces of bodies were probably never found as the tons of debris were

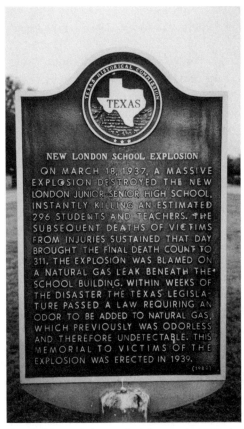

The Texas Historical Commission marked the spot in 1989. Author photo.

hauled out. Since all the records were destroyed by the blast, no one knows exactly how many people were in the school. While estimates ran as high as 600, 277 names were inscribed on the granite cenotaph. The director of the museum believes that the correct number is 319, based on county records. In the confusion, many parents who came across their children's bodies, gravely injured or dead, may have simply picked them up and carried them away with them. Many parents who became convinced that their children were dead may have left the area or never bothered to report their losses to anyone in authority.

By 2:00 A.M., while workers were using acetylene torches to free the study hall teacher, Pearline Gary, an attempt was made to take stock of the situation. It was found to be impossible. One hundred fifty bodies had been taken to Henderson alone. Other bodies had been taken to Kilgore, Jacksonville, Tyler, and Overton. The hospitals in those towns were already beyond capacity. Children were being taken to doctor's offices, churches, and legion halls.

At 4:00 A.M. the workers reached the last room, located over the center of the explosion. Parts of what were presumed to be twenty-seven different bodies were recovered.

At 5:00 A.M. a thunderstorm broke. The school ground became an ocean of red mud. Despite exhaustion and the deluge, the workers continued until the last piece of rubble was carried out. Over two thousand tons of wreckage had been hauled from the school grounds. Seven more bodies were found just before daylight.

Some men, unable to rest after the sheer horror of their ordeal, simply went to the cemeteries and began to dig graves.

New London's grief became the grief of the world as the news spread. Within hours an unmatched outpouring of love and sympathy for the death of such precious innocence came to the people of Rusk County. Both President Franklin D. Roosevelt and his wife Eleanor, one of the most influential women of the twentieth century, sent personal messages accompanied by promises "that everything possible will be done to relieved the injured."

From Germany, despite tensions that would soon plunge the entire Northern Hemisphere into a battle that would kill millions of innocent children, Chancellor Adolph Hitler sent a telegram ensuring the people of "my and the German people's sincere sympathy." From Australia, from France, from Spain, from Argentina came telegrams. From the Fukuoka Girls' High

School in Japan came a telegram and later a scroll that read in part, "[We are] praying for the repose of the victim's souls, with deepest sympathy."

Perhaps the saddest report came from the front page of the *Henderson Daily News*, Sunday, March 21, after the explosion on Thursday. "Five of those little victims of this tragedy were members of the distribution department of this newspaper. They would have brought your copy . . . to your home. They won't bring your *News* this morning. These words cannot be written without tears streaming from the eyes of this writer."

Just as the absolute number of dead will never be known, the absolute truth of what caused the terrible explosion is still open to question. It is known that from the time of the construction of the school until early in 1937, New London had purchased natural gas from a commercial gas company. Then Superintendent Shaw and the school board had discontinued that service. Shaw had instructed a custodian to "sink an unused pipe below the floor and cap it." Later he speculated about whether that line had been correctly closed.

New London had tapped into a "free" gas line that ran adjacent to the school. Throughout East Texas this was common practice. Gas received in this manner was "wet" or "residue." It could not be legally sold, but Parade, H. L. Hunt's gas company, "allowed" the area residents to "covertly" tap into the supply since it would be burned as waste anyway. Again, whether or not the tap was properly done is open to speculation.

Ironically, the "richest little school" in Texas could easily have afforded the monthly gas bill. They chose to save a little money. Of course, the school board president, Mr. Reagan, testified that all the board members were fully aware that natural gas had to be handled properly. They had installed a "new standard commercial regulator that held pressure down to a rate similar to commercial supplies, and had installed a screening device to remove contaminants."

Some people suspected the gas radiators in use in all the schoolrooms. Attached to gas jets by flexible hoses, their connections were unprotected in all the classrooms. They were easily jostled by the children, as well as by the custodial staff in their daily cleanings. However, the explosion did not occur in just one room.

Because of the totality of the destruction that occurred in all parts of the building constructed over the crawl space, it is most often concluded that gas from a leak beneath the floors filled the space and seeped up into the walls and into the classroom themselves. The spark jumping in the shop class struck exactly the proper mixture to turn the schoolhouse into a bomb.

Further substantiation for this theory comes from the fact that additional portions of the building, such as the gymnasium, constructed over a foundation set flat on the ground were relatively undamaged.

People accustomed to the litigious society of the latter part of the twentieth century will have trouble appreciating the thinking of men in the early half. The fathers of the lost ones were oil field workers whose jobs involved heights, fire, toxic substances, and heavy machinery with constantly moving parts. To those pragmatic souls, an accident was an accident. Investigators for the state legislature concluded, "The source of the gas supply is irrelevant to the cause of the explosion, and the results would have been approximately the same under similar conditions regardless of the natural gas used."

While the twenty-first century might see millions of dollars in lawsuits bankrupting the school board, the school administration, H. L. Hunt, Ross Sterling, the Parade and Humble oil companies, New London, the East Texas oil field, Rusk County, and even the state of Texas itself, the attitude was that nothing could bring the children back. No attempt was ever made to bring suit or to attach blame to any entities.

Within days a double irony was revealed. On April 13, 1937, five days before the tragedy of New London, the Texas House, urged by Steve Hawley, chief engineer of the Texas Fire Insurance Department, had introduced H.B. No. 1017, which required the introduction of a malodorant agent into natural-gas supplies. The bill had been greeted with some hoots and snickers about "malodorous gas," but Hawley's case was taken seriously. Since natural gas was colorless, odorless, and tasteless, no one could detect it in a classroom or, for that matter, a bedroom where a gas space heater might be left on low for the night.

The bill passed the House 100–3. The Senate was dragging its feet until Carolyn Jones, one of the very few New London fifth graders to survive, spoke to the joint session of the legislature one week after the explosion. Her tearful speech brought about the desired legislation. Once the full import of the tragedy was studied, two more bills addressing standards for installation, inspection, and maintenance were introduced. On May 7 all three passed 29–0.

The state of Texas snapped into action to make certain that no more children would die as the children of New London had died.

For the rest of the term, schools in the East Texas oil field heated with "wet" gas were closed on days the superintendent deemed the weather too cold for them to attend. By the time the schools resumed in September, the legislative bills were fully implemented.

For New London itself, school began again eleven days after the disaster. The primary grades attended classrooms in their building only slightly damaged from the blast. Temporary buildings were put up for the rest of the survivors. The first day back was "like one big party." Everybody was so happy to be alive and so happy to see their friends alive. They flew into each other's arms and hugged and cried as if they had emerged from a terrible nightmare.

So many of them had not been sure they would ever get back to school again.

The cenotaph to the children and teachers. Author photo.

The school as it has been rebuilt on the grounds of the old. Author photo.

The people of New London, still as rich in wealth but infinitely poorer in all the ways that counted, commissioned a magnificent cenotaph. They built a much bigger educational facility with everything that money could buy. It sits on the grounds of the old school.

Across the street, in a drugstore where New London teens used to congregate for sodas after school, is a tearoom and museum. Its director and chief docent is Mollie Sealy Ward, who as a fifth grader danced the Mexican hat dance in the gymnasium and was then dismissed to sit on the bus rather than go back to class where she would perhaps have died two minutes later. Her old friends drop in to eat lunch, and visitors come to remember one of Texas's greatest disasters.

"New London"
(A gentle, welcoming tune)

It happened sixty years ago.
It could be you've forgot.
A spark jumped from a bandsaw
In London's schoolhouse shop,
And those who could remember
Were left with nightmare scenes
When a terrible explosion blew
The school to smithereens.

In the manner of brave Texans,
We buried those who died.
We mourned and built the school again
And put it all aside.
Friends grew up. The years flew by,
And suddenly we were old.
It shouldn't be what happened here
Never would be told.

Of course, there's a memorial,
But the statue's something cold.
People need to see their faces
And hear their stories told.
We'll build here a museum
About the town and such
And people from around the world
Who sympathized so much.

With Mollie Ward to spur us on,
No one dared to shirk.
The town was all behind us
As they helped us do the work.
Now, we have a place of memory
In the drugstore that was then.
A new school stands across the way.
Our grandkids can drop in.

Don't pass us by, we beg you.
We want you all to see
The scroll from far away Japan
They sent in sympathy.
A little bit of history
And the memories that we share,
Our friends will be remembered,
When we're no longer there.

Yes, our friends will be remembered
When we're no longer there.

10

THE DEATH OF THE RIVER

In the summer of 2001, the Rio Grande ran dry a quarter of a mile from the Gulf of Mexico.

The day the river of legend and lore disappeared into a dry, windswept sandbar, people came down to mourn. Some of them picked up pieces of driftwood—oh, primitive implements—to scratch out a symbolic path onward to the sea.

One hundred yards inland from the Gulf, these pathetic engineers started from a tepid pool ringed by dead and stinking fish. The creatures had been trapped and suffocated when the water they had swum in became stagnant and overheated.

Also around the pool and farther back in the trickle of water coming south lay some of the detritus of desperation:

Old tires are used by nonswimmers to cross illegally from Tamaulipas, Mexico, into Cameron County, Texas. Tractor tires are the favorites because of their size. The northern banks farther upriver near the town of Mission are lined with them.

Cast-off shoes are there as well. Some of their shoelaces are tied together, perhaps by the same people who hoped they'd live to don them when they reached the Texas side.

Most pathetic are the plastic water jugs. What fierce determination a man must have to tie two empty gallon jugs together, slip the cord across his chest and under his armpits, and make himself a pair of crude water wings. What must be the depths of his desperation?

Because of the high, slippery banks of the lower Rio Grande and the sluggish-seeming flow, it is no easy swim. Instead, it is deceptively dangerous.

Ill-equipped men and sometimes women wade into the river and strike out. With a dawning sense of horror, they realize that they are not going to be able to kick easily to the other side. Not only are they not directly across from where they started, but they are not even able to cross. Instead, as panic grows inside them, they are pushed, sometimes slowly, sometimes rapidly, downstream, twisted around and around, swirled back toward the bank they came from. With no idea how to swim, they exhaust themselves, their hands slip, they separate from their source of buoyancy, and they drown.

How many people who have never learned to swim dare the river every year is unknown. Sometimes, their bodies lodge in waterlogged snags, reaching upward from the brown-green depths. No one comes to fish them out. They are food for fish until their bones disappear into the silt. Sometimes the bodies tangle in the hydrilla and water hyacinths so thick that purple gallinule and other water birds walk upon them.

These plants are a constant problem in the river nowadays and not just for swimmers. The river, so depleted by dams, reservoirs, and evaporation along its length, hasn't the strength to tear these plants out by the roots and sweep them along toward the Gulf. Instead, they win the battle, and the river slows still more. These are alien plants introduced years ago by accident and lack of environmental understanding. Now they have to be cleared periodically by giant mowing machines that scythe their way through the water. So fast-growing are they that if the machines are left in the river a day or two, the machines themselves may be trapped. The layers of plants twine and twist their way around the propeller shafts and clog the mechanisms, and men's best efforts are frustrated.

Did the small group of concerned citizens know what they were looking at when they tried to encourage the river to run freely again? Did they actually think they might encourage the river whose problems began in the Rocky Mountains in faraway Colorado?

Tragically, the situation they confronted was not unique. It had occurred several times during the 1950s when a decade-long drought gripped the entire Southwest. In 1951 the Rio Grande stopped flowing through Brownsville for 193 days. In 1953, the worst year on record, only 11.59 inches of rain fell in the Laguna Atascosa National Wildlife Refuge a few miles north of the river mouth.

While the drought of 2001 was bad, it would not have been sufficient to cause the water to disappear underground. Man himself has done that.

Much wanton waste and abuse of natural resources have occurred in the last half of the twentieth century, a supposedly enlightened time when the citizenry should have known better. Now the river has run dry again.

The problem is more than alarming. It is frightening. Mexico and Texas are now locked in a struggle that is literally life and death for thousands of people, animals, and plants. An entire ecosystem is being rapidly destroyed.

Water overuse and burgeoning populations in its watershed have turned the Rio Grande into a mere trickle of its former great self. The third or fourth longest river on the continent, depending on how it is measured, the partial boundary between two of the three great countries that make up North America has become an ongoing disaster.

What happened to turn the Big River into a catastrophe?

Unlike a lake or an ocean, a river is a body of water that follows the principal of gravity. It flows downward from high mountains where snow melts in bright sunlight.

Although the Rio Grande's origins are nearly nineteen hundred miles away from its end point in the Gulf of Mexico, it would be coursing like the Mississippi, pushed by the thousands of gallons flowing behind it . . . if the thousands of gallons were allowed to flow freely.

A low snowpack in the San Juan Mountains, part of the Rocky Mountain chain in southern Colorado, was the first nail in the coffin of the ecological disaster that the people in the lower Rio Grande valley witnessed firsthand. Tragically, it was only the beginning.

Water taken from the river close to its source has recently been tested for trace elements. Discovered were arsenic, mercury, copper, selenium, and antimony—a witches' brew of poisonous sediments. Some are from long-closed mines; some are from mines in current operation. It is a shame, a disgrace, but what is put into the water farther down is infinitely worse.

Bearing its first noxious burden, the water ripples on the first part of its journey to Albuquerque, New Mexico. It is a delight for all to see because it is primarily a spectacular set of gorges. The most famous and most often visited is the Rio Grande Gorge west of Taos, New Mexico. There the visitor stands on a high bridge and gazes down, down into a river so far below that it looks like a mere trickle—a stream to jump across. Yet, whitewater froths on the ripples around boulders in the far-distant stream.

Due southwest from Taos, bypassing Santa Fe, it flows past Los Alamos

The bridge over the Rio Grande Gorge west of Taos, New Mexico. Author photo.

where atomic energy research and development are always in progress. The facility must dispose of its waste somewhere. The river is a likely source. The sort of waste it puts into the water is open to speculation.

In downtown Albuquerque, the river flows under the Central Avenue Bridge, where riders see some of the horrors of modern urban river treatment. Banked by cottonwoods but in no way concealed are steel tank traps wired and chained together, ostensibly to prevent erosion. The largest city in New Mexico displays little interest in beautifying the riverbanks in its very heart.

The town was founded there because of the fresh, clear water of the Rio Grande. The present population of Albuquerque seems to care nothing for the river except to take its water from it and to prevent it from encroaching in any way upon their land.

Perhaps that's for the best. The water is sluggish and cloudy. Anyone actually wanting to take a swim in it would have to think about the residue that is being washed down from the mountains at Rio Rancho where the Intel plant returns its used water.

The company boasts that its return water is perfectly safe, that it is "almost" as pure as when it was taken out. Although many concerned Albuquerque environmentalists raise their voice against Intel and its prac-

The Rio Grande from the Gorge Bridge. Author photo.

tices, the state's largest private industrial employer of fifty-two hundred New Mexicans and the state's largest corporate income tax payer has so far tipped the scales in its favor. Who cares about a slightly "milky" look?

Thereafter, the land flattens on the high desert, and the river runs south to Socorro, only a few miles from the White Sands Missile Range, where the first atomic bomb test was conducted. Within this proximity a traveler might pause as he gazes at the smooth-flowing river to consider atomic debris from fallout and the nature of radioactive half-life. Who knows what trace amounts of Strontium 90 and Uranium 235 might set Geiger counters clicking if a sample were brought into a lab? Despite the passage of more than half a century, are active isotopes slowly leaking into the river?

Still rolling along, evaporating as it passes through the hot desert sun

The Rio Grande north of Albuquerque, New Mexico. Author photo.

and dry air, the river reaches Truth or Consequences, a town named for a ridiculous radio quiz program. A few miles south, not one but two dams have been built to impound the water for irrigation. At that point, still hundreds of miles from the Gulf, the Rio Grande becomes subject to the control and the hands of men.

In 1906 Mexico and the United States signed a treaty to control the river they shared. The result was the Elephant Butte Dam, opened in 1916 to detain the water on its way south. The reservoir that resulted was not only long and narrow but shallow. When there seemed to be enough water for all, it was a wonder of modern engineering.

Today, it is judged a high-evaporation reservoir that should be abandoned for water storage in favor of aquifers or deeper reservoirs. Yet, it continues to be used while thousands of gallons of precious resource disappear into thin air.

Its twin, the Caballo Dam, was added with a canal project. The existing riverbanks were to be strengthened and in many places straightened so the floods that had resulted in damage and crop losses would be eliminated. That these floods in the long term also spread loam across the land and contributed to the accumulation of groundwater in aquifers was thought to be less important than the short-term control. That the land requires more and more artificial fertilization and the aquifers are being drawn down is beginning to bother people who care about the future, but their alarm is so far insufficient to effect change.

Despite the treaty the Elephant Butte and Caballo water releases created tension between the United States and Mexico in the early decades of the twentieth century. Mexico was guaranteed sixty thousand acre-feet of irrigation water annually to her farmers south of the river around Juárez. Of course, during low snow melt-off in Colorado this figure was much reduced. What Mexico counted as her fair share did not appear. The U.S. failure to provide has now come back to haunt the river in the twenty-first century.

The Mesilla and the ninety-mile-long El Paso–Juárez valleys should be productive and efficiently run. Together they constitute one of the oldest irrigated areas in New Mexico. The oldest towns in Texas—Ysleta, Socorro, and San Elizario—hug the riverbanks there. Everyone who lives there should be happy.

But problems began when urbanites saw these idyllic rural communities and wanted to live there. People who were not stewards of the land moved into this paradise. For their daily lives they required more and more water that had nothing to do with farming. Less water could therefore be diverted into irrigation ditches. Consequently, these oldest of Texas towns, which have been models of productivity and good management for centuries, now have a water problem even on the banks of the river.

Texas and Mexico have yet to address the problems that they know exist. The major one is, of course, there will never be enough water to satisfy everyone. As soon as more water was controlled and released at regular periods, more people moved in and needed it for their crops. A megaplex comprising two thickly populated cities—El Paso, Texas, and Ciudad Juárez, Chihuahua—now lives with a constant water crisis. The Rio Grande, or the Río Bravo del Norte, the river with two names scarcely has water enough for one.

Between these cities all pretense of a river has given way to a canal with cement banks, high chain-link fences, and tangles of barbed wire angled outward to keep people from climbing across.

While El Paso takes only 40 percent of its water from the river, its sources in the end will run out. Plans are being made to purchase water ranches, perhaps from the panhandle, where the precious substance will be extracted from groundwater or aquifers. How this groundwater will replace itself is a question that no politicians or water managers have solutions for at this point.

Drawing aquifer overdrafts at a higher rate than the rate of replenishment is already becoming a problem in many drought-stricken cities in the West where water rationing occurs every summer. The people in the cities do not understand or do not want to understand that water is swiftly becoming a limited resource. Intent on gratifying their own needs, they appear to care little that the river has still to travel through a thousand miles of fertile land to reach the Gulf. Where will all the water downstream come from?

In the not-too-distant future, urban populations will fight with farmers and ranchers for water. The farmers and ranchers will lose, and a way of life along the riverbanks will die. Of course, the crops and cattle these people raise and sell will be gone as well, which will mean less food for the ever-burgeoning population that requires it. The war is one that no one wins.

South of El Paso lie the great Chihuahua Desert and the Big Bend National Park. Over this distance the river receives relatively little stress because few people live in one of the hottest deserts on the continent. At the same time it receives little water because very little rain falls.

In the Big Bend the river has actually stopped flowing. The river guides that took Lady Bird Johnson through the Santa Elena Canyon to publicize her beautification program in the 1960s have gone out of business. Where there is no river, no one needs a guide.

In the canyon the river turns into a series of isolated pools separated by dry white gravel. There is no flow. In fact, the Big Bend is now listed among the top-ten endangered national parks, based on degradation of the river as well as air pollution. To save itself, the river has gone underground. Somewhere beneath its bed it sneaks toward the sea, seeping silently through the gravel. But a river without a flow baking in the sun of Mariscal Canyon in April is neither *río* nor *grande*. It is a disaster.

And as for the birds, fish, wildlife, and river flora, they have no chance to survive. Without a vote, they are doomed.

Unlike the Mississippi, which receives water from all the rivers in the United States between the Rockies and the Appalachians, the Rio Grande receives water from only two. Not until the town of Presidio does the Rio Grande receive a fresh supply of water from its first major tributary.

The Río Conchos rises on the Continental Divide in the heart of the Sierra Madre Occidentals and converges on the small town that frequently holds the record for posting the hottest summer temperature in the nation.

During the protracted drought of the 1950s, the Río Conchos dried up for twenty consecutive days. Five million citizens in northern Mexico were without drinking water or any means of getting it, except when the government hauled it in in tanker trucks and rationed it by the jug. What will be their future in a very short time?

To reduce farmers' water is to reduce their lives. In Mexico after centuries of pre-Columbian farming techniques, the productivity of the land has been reduced to mere subsistence. If the water necessary to maintain even a meager subsistence is no more, these neglected people have nowhere to go. A disaster of mythic proportions is in the future south of the border.

Today the Río Conchos is also a river in serious trouble. The first hydroelectric dam, La Boquilla, was completed in 1910 by a team of Canadian engineers during the height of the Mexican Revolution. Its reservoir provided water for agricultural expansion and a decent living for thousands of small farmers. Farther down the river into the desert, two other high dams, Madero and Luis L. León, further control the river.

The experiences of the farmers in Texas and New Mexico were repeated on the banks of the Conchos. Their resources were sold for a short-term gain that greatly weakened the river.

First, teams of loggers moved in and cut down the trees at the river's headwaters, significantly reducing its flow. No sooner had the trees disappeared than another group of people moved into the pleasant valleys while the water still flowed freely, although not so freely as before. All along the river's banks they cleared away lush riverside habitat or took so much water from the river that the habitat dried up. More evaporation has followed.

Along with river loss came the blight of the northern regions of Mexico. Entrepreneurs set up *maquiladoras*, small, labor-intensive factories that employ over one million Mexicans.

Primarily women, they work in approximately four thousand *maquiladoras* for U.S., Japanese, and European employers. Girls between the ages of fourteen and twenty are paid as little as fifty cents an hour to work ten hours a day, six days a week. They live in substandard housing, mostly shacks that create slums on the edges of towns like Ciudad Juárez, Nuevo Laredo, Reynosa, and Matamoros. In sight of the river, their factories' source for water, they often live without running water and electricity. Because the *maquiladoras* have been thrown up with such indecent haste, they have inadequate wastewater disposal. The river becomes polluted with industrial wastewater as well as untreated, raw sewage.

The girls are exploited at every turn by their bosses and the system that allows these sweatshops to exist. Since the North American Free Trade Agreement (NAFTA), the number of these factories has increased because taxes and custom fees are almost nonexistent throughout the continent.

What will Mexico do with the increasing population in semidesert areas? What will the United States do? The problems are becoming unmanageable. What will these girls do when the water runs out, and they no longer have jobs? Their employers will surely close the *maquiladoras* without a thought as to how and where these young women will go next.

Mexico's failure to let its promised share of water flow into the Rio Grande has created hard feelings between the two countries. Today Boquillas, Madero, and Luis León reservoirs have a billion cubic meters of water stored. Americans look at their own water problems and then at the stored water. They want their share as entitled to them by treaty, but Mexican farmers cannot forget how Americans kept their releases low from Elephant Butte and Caballo reservoirs.

Although a billion cubic meters sounds like an ocean, it is not much water to be distributed among five million citizens in northern Mexico. Because of the dry years and the destruction of the watershed, the reservoirs contain only 31.8 percent of their capacity.

The Rio Grande might be dry through the Big Bend's canyons. Farmers in South Texas might be crying for water. Presidents George Bush and Vicente Fox may make agreements until the stars fall from the sky, but the people of Mexico will not give up their water with so little of it remaining. They cannot let it go, and we may not be able to live without it.

A person looking at a map might trace the northward curve of the Rio Grande out of the Big Bend and think that there is hope for more water. South of the little town of Langtry, the Pecos River enters the Rio Grande on an arm of the International Amistad Reservoir.

The Amistad and Falcón reservoirs were conceived in 1932 and designed to have storage capacities of five million or so acre-feet. The first stage of the project was the Lower Rio Grande Valley Flood Control Project, which strengthened and raised levees, dredged the channel, and created floodways. In 1944 the United States and Mexico committed to the construction of the two great dams.

The Pecos originates on the western slope of the Sangre de Cristo Mountains and runs south through the town of Taos, New Mexico. The snowfall there is great for skiing, so the Pecos gets a good start. Tumbling out of the mountains, it runs like a younger sister parallel to the Rio Grande almost the entire length of the state of New Mexico before it crosses into Texas and cuts through the Guadalupe Mountains.

Less than a century ago, the Pecos was sixty-five to one hundred feet wide and seven to ten feet deep. The current was swift and crossings were few. In fact, most trail herds would travel miles along its banks to get to the famous Horsehead Crossing, probably located about forty-five miles northeast of Fort Stockton. Cattle driven at least two days without water would begin to hurry when they smelled the river. Horses stepped out eagerly. Many cowboys swore they could smell it too. Water is life for everything.

Now the Pecos is totally controlled. The only times it runs are when releases are made from the reservoirs for irrigation for the half million acres along its banks. Such an agricultural paradise has attracted more farmers than the current releases from the river can supply. Rather than count themselves failures, the farmers are being forced to use groundwater for their four hundred thousand acres of crops, including the famous Pecos cantaloupes.

But recent years have brought a horrible awakening. The groundwater may well be irreplaceable. The farmers of Texas have brought suit against the farmers of New Mexico for the release of more water. The wars between the states have begun all over again. How much water the Pecos lets into the Rio Grande may be grounds for another suit someday soon.

South of Amistad is the town of Del Rio. Controlled by the dam, the Rio Grande courses southeast fifty-six miles to the little town of Eagle Pass on the Texas side and the town of Piedras Negras on the Mexican side. Below Eagle Pass, the road leaves the river to travel alone for nearly a hundred miles more. The distance is too short.

At the river's next destination, the infusion of water is woefully insufficient. At Amistad, the inhabitants of Laredo, Texas, and Nuevo Laredo, Tamaulipas, may be doomed. The two towns' unparalleled growth has turned them into cities. Thirty years ago the discovery of a huge field of natural gas brought prosperity to the region. A primarily agrarian society was supplanted by one based on industrial wealth with its industrial problems, in particular industrial pollution.

NAFTA has brought its own kind of trouble along the southern bank. As at the entry of the Conchos, the Pecos infusion of water has brought the *maquiladoras* mushrooming like weeds. The river is particularly foul here. The factories have few standards with which to comply, and the shanties of the workers have only the most primitive disposal of waste.

Unfortunately, all these people and their industries depend on the Rio

Grande for 100 percent of their water. Even the uninformed know that the situation can scarcely be worse or more dangerous. Where will the citizens of these two cities go when their water is gone?

After Laredo no more large tributaries enter the Rio Grande from the American side. The Río Salado enters from the Mexican side into an arm of the last big dam on the Rio Grande, International Falcón Reservoir dedicated in 1953 by President Dwight D. Eisenhower. Farther downstream the San Juan enters north of Rio Grande City, less than a hundred miles from the mouth of the river. However, the San Juan's water is controlled by a dam that retains a reservoir several miles from the river.

If the people of Tamaulipas need the water, the people of Cameron, Hidalgo, Willacy, and Starr counties can kiss any substantial release goodbye.

The lower Rio Grande valley of Texas, comprising the four small counties named above, is a jewel of agriculture. In 1929, John H. Shary founded the Texas citrus fruit industry there. Publicity of that time referred to it as the Winter Gardens. One of the last frontiers of Texas and the United States was turned into a tropical paradise of black, waxy, delta soil left by the alluvial flooding of the Rio Grande on its way to the Gulf.

Ironically, even as farms and orchards were taking advantage of all this natural bounty, they couldn't help complaining that they couldn't control the river. More dams, reservoirs, and treaties between states and nations were created. The effort to control became a hodgepodge of conflicting rules and regulations.

With the mechanization of farming through tractors to pull plows, discs, and harrows, the invention of not one but two types of mechanized cotton pickers, and the development of combines to harvest grain sorghums, the small family farm disappeared. One hundred twenty acres had never been more than subsistence living. Now it gave way to businessmen whose business was agribusiness.

Farms were being planted by sixteen-row plows that could plant two hundred acres a day. A one-thousand-acre farm could be planted in a week by one man. An acre of cotton no longer took one hundred fifty man-hours to pick. A cotton picker could do it in 6.5 man-hours. In order to use a cotton picker efficiently, defoliants were used to clear the trash out of the cotton picker's way, dropping dead leaves and weeds to the ground where they could be plowed under to enrich the soil. Three kinds of herbicides—

preplanting, preemergent, and postemergent—kept the weeds out of the cotton.

The line of rickety cotton trailers waiting at the small, independent gin disappeared. They were replaced by huge modules of compacted cotton covered by tarps waiting in the field on pallets to be collected by a super-sized gin as their turn came to be processed. Today, such gins operate for months.

Even farmers were no longer independent (if they ever had been). Loan officers at banks and credit institution officers gave advice on planting and harvesting. Private enterprise stepped in to fill the demands for goods and services. Implements, seeds, fertilizers, and chemicals became just some of the peripherals. All these people depended upon the farmer, and indirectly the river, for their livelihoods.

Federal and state researchers and colleges and universities manned experiment stations. Their jobs and grants depended on the success of the farmers' crops.

A government bureaucracy was created to organize and regulate everything. Farmers tried desperately to hold their own against people who knew nothing about their problems. The American Farm Bureau Federation, the National Farmers' Union, and the American Agriculture Association were organized.

The industry kept growing and growing. Texas products left ports on the Gulfs of Mexico and California to find their way to China and to Africa, to Europe and to South America—anywhere people could be found to work in sweatshops for lower wages than the *maquiladora* girls. The web became so tight that no one could be allowed to fail.

And yet the seeds of the web's failure—the mightiest disaster of all—the one affecting not just thousands, but millions, of people may be in the very near future. The millions of people living along the banks of the rivers may cause the river to fail because they will demand more and more water.

The river will have no more to give.

The Rio Grande flows very slowly in the last hundred miles of its journey. It is now stressed to its very banks. It is dry in some places. In short, it has been turned into little better than a drainage ditch.

Meanwhile, farmland is disappearing at an alarming rate because of subdivisions being built for retirement communities. The population of Texas is estimated to reach thirty-seven million by 2050. In the 1950s the population of the lower Rio Grande valley was closer to four hundred thousand. It has already increased to 1.2 million. Now in the next fifty years, it is expected to more than double to three million.

Some pessimists believe that before the river runs out of water the farms, orchards, and ranches will have disappeared. All that will remain are the houses with bright green lawns and exotic water-slurping plants. If anything, the residents of those homes are the seeds of their own disaster. What will happen to them when the river runs dry?

In 1997 President Bill Clinton selected the Rio Grande as one of fourteen American Heritage Rivers. It is a river with a rich heritage. But the rampant misuse of the water and the land around it, if continued unabated, will destroy the river itself. The heritage that came to us will be no more. What will we have to leave our children?

Just recently the people of the Rio Grande valley have come to realize that the whole ecosystem will be irrevocably gone if something is not done. Funds were needed to purchase and preserve tracts of land for a wildlife corridor extending from the gulf to Falcón Reservoir. In 1990 a group came together to establish a contest that they hoped would generate cash.

The contest would be for the most beautiful photographs of wildlife managing to hold on to their tiny territories despite encroachment from all sides. At the end of the contest, the winners' photographs would be published in a book.

The group further hoped that pictures, when displayed and published, would educate the public to the beauty of the land. And, finally, they hoped that even people with pieces of land as small as a backyard would conserve what habitat they could to allow birds, plants, and animals to flourish.

The plan has succeeded beyond its own hopes. In 1994 the first contest drew 90 percent of its photographers from South Texas. The first book sold out completely, and copies, when offered for resale, brought twice and three times their original price.

Ten years later the fifth contest drew 90 percent of its participants from elsewhere in the United States as well as from foreign countries. The big draw is the $150,000 in prizes donated by conservation-conscious citizens and businesses. The books with the contest winners' photos make wonderful gifts as well as collector's pieces. The profits from their sale go into a fund to purchase land to complete and expand the proposed corridor.

As more people have become part of this effort, the results have attracted nationwide attention. In many cases this habitat and its plants and animals exist only in this small pocket in the United States. In some cases they may exist nowhere else in the world. And the race to save them may already be a losing one.

For example, two small wild cats—the ocelot, which looks like a small leopard with big eyes, and the jaguarundi, which looks like a small mountain lion with a tawny pelt—live in this area. In 2002 the annual photo contest offered a Rare Cat Prize of $5,000 to the photographer and the landowner who took the winning picture of either animal.

Not one picture was taken.

Of course, these animals are very wary—perhaps too wary to be photographed. Surely, they cannot have vanished altogether.

That the two governments; the agribusiness communities; the peasant farmers; the cities, towns, villages, and *colónias*; the *maquiladoras*; and all the other entities that line the river's banks may not be able to come to any sort of solution sits like the specter at the feast in all negotiations between the two countries. If the sister states of Texas and New Mexico are in conflict, what chance do hostile, suspicious countries have of reaching a solution? Abused as they are, how long can the rivers continue to run?

The conflicts inherent in water rationing involve life and death. The rivals for the precious drink of life are powerful: urban versus rural; indigenous and Native American people versus city populations; and on a broader scale, international coalitions of economic developers against hard-line environmentalists.

Furthermore, given the adversarial relationship that the United States has shared with Mexico over the last one hundred fifty years, any sort of agreement is difficult to achieve and even harder to maintain.

Recommendations for sustainable water use and the apportionment of it to the parties who must use it to survive make up a long list. Among them is the creation of a binational water market and a water bank to buy and sell water, thereby encouraging conservation and wise water use.

To improve the quality of the water, the first priority is to curb contamination. Contamination of the water by fecal matter has risen alarmingly. Cameron County, where the river empties into the Gulf, has seen a rise of 400 percent in cases of Hepatitis A in the years since NAFTA was enacted.

To improve irrigation techniques and agricultural management, one recommendation is that crop and climate compatibility should be brought more into alignment. Instead of growing sugar cane, which requires large infusions of water, farmers should grow crops such as grain sorghums that can sustain yields on dry land.

Above all, population growth must be kept at sustainable rates. To allow the population of El Paso to double every twenty-five years is a crime against nature. It cannot be sustained and eventually people will indeed start dying without water.

If they are not already doing so.

A float trip down the river fifty miles or so from its mouth reveals the same old tires abandoned on the bank, the same plastic gallon jugs, the same shoes, the same makeshift rafts, the same detritus of dreams. Some are on the U.S. side; some are on the Mexican.

Did their riders make it? Did they survive the deceptive river currents to make it to a new life?

What irony! They could have traveled a few miles farther south along its banks and walked across on dry land. But, of course, they could not wait.

A further irony is that the rich future they believe awaits them, the good life with jobs for everyone, may be a vanished dream in the very near future. The nightmare will be when a mighty river is gone forever and the whole world is one step closer to becoming a desert.

And that will be the worst disaster of all.

"Rio Grande"
(3/4 time, country-western-ballad style)

From the mountains of old Colorado,
When the snows melt right early in spring,
Bright trickles of water come flowing,
A-joining to cleave through the plain.

Come ripples, come rivulets, come rapids, through sand.
The blue Rio Grande's the lord of the land.

Millenniums' snow melts eternal
And pushes the sand toward its flanks.
The plain has become a wide channel,
And the river is born in its banks.

The water cuts deep to the heart of the Earth,
Where it cools the volcanoes of old
Through layers of limestone and granite,
Through obsidian, sandstone, and gold,

Slicing gorges and scraping out canyons,
Creating the o'erhanging cliffs,
A-twisting and falling on seaward,
And watering the land where it drifts.

Come ripples, come rivulets, come rapids, through sand.
The brown Rio Grande's the lord of the land.

Its wildness divides two great nations,
One to the south and one north.
Its freedom and power they must harness
To pull from the land all its worth.

So they dammed it to keep it from flooding.
They straightened its tortuous bend.
The loam that it reaped from the mountains,
They channeled it where they would send.

A free-flowing outlaw no longer,
It's tamed to the uses of man,
Who water their crops and their cattle
And send less and less where they can.

The ripples, the rivulets, the rapids are gone.
Last drops disappear from the land.
No water flows out of its mouth to the sea.
Now sadly, its throat's choked with sand.

A prophetic moment strikes terror.
It raises our dire, deepest fears.
For the death of a river so mighty
Cuts the heart far too deeply for tears.

READINGS ABOUT
TEXAS DISASTERS

Archer, Jane. *Texas Indian Myths and Legends*. Plano, TX: Republic of Texas Press, 2000.

Baden, Ira J., as told to Robert H. Parham. "My 45 Seconds Inside the Tornado," *The Saturday Evening Post,* July 11, 1953, 17–19, 74–78.

Banks, Suzy. "Rio de Enero," *Texas Monthly* (January 2004): 58–61.

Barker, Tim, et al. "Retooling NASA Won't Be Simple," *Valley Morning Star,* August 31, 2003, A10.

Blaney, Betsy. "Algae Blooms Devastate Fish Populations in Many Texas Lakes," *Valley Morning Star,* July 21, 2003, B4.

Bridis, Ted. "New Threat to Shuttle Discovered," *Valley Morning Star,* June 13, 2003, A4.

Cantrell, Mark, and Donald Vaughan. *Sixteen Minutes from Home: The Columbia Space Shuttle Tragedy.* Boca Raton, FL: AMI Books, 2003.

Cappella, Chris. "Tornadoes Are Earth's Most Violent Storms," *USA Today,* at www .usatoday.comweather/resources/basics/twist0.htm (accessed March 10, 2004).

Cartwright, Frederick F. *Disease and History.* New York: New American Library, 1974.

Chapman, Jim. "The Rio Grande: Dying a Piece at a Time," *Mesquite Review* (June/ July 2003): 51.

"City Becoming Normal," *San Antonio Evening News,* September 12, 1921, 1, 2.

"Cleanup and Reconstruction Command," *San Antonio Express,* September 12, 1921, 1, 2.

"Damage Caused by High Water of September, 1921, Can Be Prevented at Cost of Less Than $3,000,000," *San Antonio Express,* November 25, 1923, n.p.

Davis, Rod. "Rio Grande *No Mas?*" *Texas Parks and Wildlife* (July 2002): 90–103.

"Dead Bodies Recovered Now Total 175," *San Antonio Evening News,* September 13, 1921, 1.

"Detention Basin on Olmos Is Vital to Check Floods," *San Antonio Express,* September 18, 1921, 1, 2.

Dethloff, Henry C., and Garry L. Nall. "Agriculture." *The Handbook of Texas Online,* at www.tsha.utexas.edu/handbook/online/articles/view/AA/amal.html (accessed Friday, March 16, 14:47:48 U.S./Central, 2004).

"Documents Show Shuttle Wing Breached More Than 3 Years Ago," *Valley Morning Star,* July 9, 2003, A5.

Dunn, Marcia. "NASA Investigator Says They Have 'Smoking Gun,'" *Valley Morning Star,* July 8, 2003, A10.

———. "NASA to Embed Shuttle Wing with Sensors," *Valley Morning Star,* December 12, 2003, A3.

"Dust in the wind," at www.atmo.ttu.edu/dust.html.

Easton, Pam. "Astronauts' Husbands Attend East Texas Shuttle Memorial," *Valley Morning Star,* February 2, 2004.

———. "Families of Columbia Crew Ready for Closure," *Valley Morning Star,* February 1, 2004.

———. "Tragedy over Texas," *Valley Morning Star,* February 1, 2004.

Fehrenbach, T. R. *Lone Star: A History of Texas and the Texans.* New York: Macmillan, 1968.

"Galveston Hurricane of 1900." *The Handbook of Texas Online,* at www.tsha.utexas.edu/handbook/online/articles/view/GG/ydg2.html (accessed Friday, August 22, 13:59:29 U.S./Central, 2003).

Graeme. "Smallpox," at www.seercom.com/bluto/science/2/immunoweb/bad/invaders/viruses/smallpox/history.html.

Hayter, Delmar J. "Pecos River." *The Handbook of Texas Online,* at www.tsha.utexas.edu/handbook/online/articles/view/PP/rnp2.html (accessed Friday, March 19, 16:37:10 U.S./Central, 2004.)

Heller, Dick D. "Rio Grande-Falcon Thorn Woodland." *The Handbook of Texas Online,* at http://222.tsha.utexas.edu/handbook/online/articles/view/RR/ryr3.html (accessed Thursday, March 25, 17:21:20 U.S./Central, 2004).

Henderson, D. A. "Smallpox: Clinical and Epidemiologic Features," at www.cdc.gov/ncidod/EID/vol5no4/henderson.html.

Henderson Daily News (facsimile montage). March 19, 1937, 1–12.

Henderson, Jim. "Depleted Rio Grande Takes Toll on Businesses, Wildlife," *Valley Morning Star,* June 22, 2003, D2.

Hickam, Homer. "NASA's Vietnam," *The Wall Street Journal,* August 29, 2003, A8.

Kaye, Ken. "Loathed, Revered Enola Gay on Display at Smithsonian," *The Valley Morning Star,* December 19, 2003, B7.

Kelton, Elmer. "The Hidden Lake," *Texas Parks and Wildlife* (July 2002): 30–39.

"Known Flood Dead 39, Score Missing," *San Antonio Express,* Sunday Morning, September 11, 1921, 1, 3.

Kolker, Claudia. "The Salty Lagoon," *Texas Parks and Wildlife* (July 2003): 50–59.

LaRoche, Clarence J. "A Disaster and Then 50 Years of Progress," *San Antonio Express,* April 8, 1974.

Linedecker, Clifford L. *Massacre at Waco, Texas.* New York: St. Martin's Paperbacks, 1993.

Lourie, Peter. *Rio Grande: From the Rocky Mountains to the Gulf of Mexico.* Honesdale, PA: Boyds Mills Press, 1999.

"Lubbock in the Dust Bowl: Lubbock, Texas Weather in the 1930s: The Letters of Dr. Allen L. Carter," at www.stmo.ttu.edu/dust/lubbockinthedustbowl.html.

Lunsford, J. Lynn, and Anne Marie Squeo. "Shuttle Probe Faults NASA Culture," *The Wall Street Journal,* August 27, 2003, A3–4.

MacWhorter, William. "Lower Rio Grande Valley National Wildlife Refuge." *The Handbook of Texas Online,* at www.tsha.utexas.edu/handbook/online/articles/view/LL/gk123.html (accessed Sunday, February 8, 5:54:20 U.S./Central, 2004).

McKinney, Larry. "Water for the Future," *Texas Parks and Wildlife* (July 2003): 21–28.

Metz, Leon C. "Rio Grande." *The Handbook of Texas Online,* at www.tsha.utexas .edu/handbook/online/articles/view/RR/rnr5.html (accessed Sunday, February 8, 67:01:09 U.S./Central, 2004).

Minutaglio, Bill. *City on Fire.* New York: HarperCollins, 2003.

Montgomery, Robert. "Water Wars: Gloomy Future for Rio Grande?" *Bassmaster.* n.p.

"NASA Determines Accident's Cause," *Valley Morning Star,* February 21, 2004, A5.

"Ogallala Aquifer," at www.npwd.org.Ogallala.html.

Olson, Lori. *New London School: In Memoriam, March 18, 1937, 3:17 P.M.* Austin, TX: Eakin Press, 2001.

Perry, Charles A. "Significant Floods in the United States during the 20th Century— WSGS Measures a Century of Floods," at http://ks.water.usgs.gov/Kansas/pubs/fact0sheets/fs.02400.html.

Pierson, Elizabeth. "Open Spaces," *Valley Morning Star,* March 15, 2004, A1, A12.

———. "No Water! How about Cash?" *Valley Morning Star,* March 18, 2004, A1, A7.

———. "Waterway under Scrutiny," *Valley Morning Star,* March 14, 2004, A1, A11–12.

Preston, Douglas. *Cities of Gold: A Journey across the American Southwest.* Albuquerque: University of New Mexico Press, 1992.

Recer, Paul. "Senators Demand Blame Game," *Valley Morning Star,* September 4, 2003, A5.

Report of the U.S.–Mexico Binational Council. *U.S.–Mexico Transboundary Water Management: The Case of the Rio Grande/Rio Bravo: Recommendations for Policymakers for the Medium and Long Term.* January 2003.

Salinas, Gilberto. "Water Relief," *Valley Morning Star,* March 16, 2004, A1, A7.

Salinas, Martín. *Indians of the Rio Grande Delta.* Austin: University of Texas Press, 1990.

"San Antonio Quickly Recovers from Disastrous Flood," *The San Antonio Light,* September 18, 1921, 1.

"San Antonio River Authority." *The Handbook of Texas Online,* at www.tsha.utexas .edu/handbook/online/articles/view/SS/mws2.html (accessed Sunday, February 8, 5:45:23 U.S./Central, 2004).

Schneider, Mike. "NASA Debates Whether to Display Shuttle Debris," *Valley Morning Star,* July 21, 2003, A8.

"SeaWiFS Observes Transport of Asian Dust over the Pacific Ocean," at http://daac .gsfc.nasa.gov.

Siegal, Ben. "S.A. Flood of '21 Recalled," *San Antonio Light,* 1, 14.

Stephens, Hugh W. *The Texas City Disaster, 1947.* Austin: University of Texas Press, 1997.

Stevenson, Mark. "Governors Stymied by Differences on Water," *Valley Morning Star,* August 9, 2003, A1, 7.

Tausch, Egon Richard. "The Branch Davidian Trial," at www.shadeslanding.com /firearms/waco.tausch.html (accessed June 14, 2003).

"Texas City Disaster." *The Handbook of Texas Online,* at www.tsha.utexas.edu/hand-book/online/aritcles/view/TT/lytl.html (accessed Friday, August 22, 14:06:46 U.S./ Central, 2003).

Texas National Guard. "Waco Disaster Operation, 11th of May, 1953 thru 20th of May, 1953," n.d.

"38 Bodies of Flood Victims Found/Search of Wreckage Continues Today/Relief Work Vigorous and Effective," *San Antonio Light,* September 11, 1921, 1, 2.

"37 Bodies Found; Dead May Total 200/Property Loss Estimated 5 Millions/Relief Work Proceeds at Rapid Pace," *San Antonio Light,* September 10, 1921, 1.

Timms, Jacqueline E. "Rio Grande Flood Control." *The Handbook of Texas Online,* at www.tsha.utexas.edu/handbook/online/articles/view/RR/mgr4.html (accessed Sunday, February 8, 5:48:42 U.S./Central, 2004).

"Tornado Project Online," at www.tornadoproject.com.

"Tornadoes." *The Handbook of Texas Online,* at www.tsha.utexas.edu/handbook/online/ articles/view/TT/ydtl.html (accessed Tuesday, August 26, 14:07:23 U.S./Central, 2003).

"Train Service Being Readjusted Again," *San Antonio Evening News,* September 14, 1921, 1.

Villegas, Daniel Cosío. *A Compact History of Mexico.* Mexico, D. F.: El Colegio de Méx-ico, 1974.

"Waco, TX," *The Handbook of Texas Online,* at www/tsha.utexas.edu/handbook/ online/articles/view/WW/hdwl.html (accessed Sunday, March 14, 15:54:37 U.S./ Central, 2004).

Wallace, Ernest, and E. Adamson Hoebel. *The Comanches, Lords of the South Plains.* Nor-man: University of Oklahoma Press, 1952.

Webb, Walter Prescott. *The Texas Rangers.* Austin: University of Texas Press, 1965.

Weems, John Edward. *A Weekend in September.* College Station: Texas A&M University Press, 1980.

Williamson, Rachel. "Desalination Funding May Be Available," *The Valley Morning Star,* July 17, 2003, A9.

Wingert, Eryn Reddell, ed. *Spirit of the Chaparral: The Magnificence of South Texas Wildlife: The Valley Land Fund Photo Contest V.* McAllen, TX: The Valley Land Fund, 2003.

Zinsser, Hans. *Rats, Lice, and History.* New York: Bantam, 1934.

ABOUT THE AUTHOR

Mona D. Sizer has firsthand experience with the disasters she writes about.

A true Texan reared in the light of the Lone Star, she has lived through two tornadoes, several hurricanes, and numerous dust storms. She grew up on a farm in the 1930s and was rescued by her determined and heroic mother from a flooded schoolyard while the rest of the children had to spend the night in the building. Trapped by a snowstorm in the Pyrenees, she and her companions spent the night with gypsies.

In her twenty-five-year career she's written fiction, history, true crime, biography, and memoir. She loves to research her subjects and sometimes spin her own experiences into the manuscript. *Texas Disasters* is her thirtieth book.